WHAT PEOPLE ARE SAYING ABOUT LET GOD LOVE YOU

"Using the complexity of human relationships, Wendy Ulrich helps us clearly see the simplicity of our relationship with God. This practical guide helps us honestly examine our deepest beliefs about Heavenly Father, thus better understanding ourselves."

> —BRAD WILCOX, BYU professor and author of *The Continuous Atonement*

"Drawing deeply from tender personal experiences, the scriptures, and key findings from her professional experience, Wendy Ulrich offers truly fresh and inspiring help with such warmth on a topic so vital to our joy: God's love. What a remarkable gift!"

> —MATTHEW AND PAIGE HOLLAND, president and first lady of Utah Valley University

"Wendy Ulrich invites us to participate in our own 'counseling session' to heal and strengthen our relationship with God. Using sound psychological principles and her own rich professional and personal experience, Dr. Ulrich both teaches and challenges us to 'let God love us'."

> —LILI DE HOYOS ANDERSON, LCSW, PhD, past president of the Association of Mormon Counselors and Psychotherapists

LET
GOD
LOVE YOU

LET
GOD
LOVE YOU

why we don't
─────────
how we can

WENDY ULRICH

DESERET
BOOK

SALT LAKE CITY, UTAH

Visit us at DeseretBook.com

Library of Congress Cataloging-in-Publication Data

Names: Ulrich, Wendy, author.
Title: Let God love you : why we don't, how we can / Wendy Ulrich.
Description: Salt Lake City, Utah : Deseret Book, [2016] | ?2016 | Includes bibliographical references and index. | Description based on print version record and CIP data provided by publisher; resource not viewed.
Identifiers: LCCN 2016008222 (print) | LCCN 2016006645 (ebook) | ISBN 9781629734507 (ebook) | ISBN 9781629722009 (paperbound)
Subjects: LCSH: God—Love—Meditations. | God (Christianity)—Love—Meditations. | Christian life—Mormon authors. | Mormon Church—Doctrines. | The Church of Jesus Christ of Latter-day Saints—Doctrines.
Classification: LCC BX8643.G63 (print) | LCC BX8643.G63 U47 2016 (ebook) | DDC 231/.6—dc23
LC record available at http://lccn.loc.gov/2016008222

Printed in the United States of America
Publishers Printing, Salt Lake City, UT

10 9 8 7 6 5 4 3 2 1

To Carla Hickman
Sister, example, cherished friend

CONTENTS

Introduction ix

SECTION ONE: THE JOURNEY OF RELATIONSHIP

Chapter 1: Why Is God Far Away? 3

Chapter 2: Stages of Committed Relationships 22

Chapter 3: A Married Wife 47

SECTION TWO: CONNECTING WITH GOD

Chapter 4: Discovering Our Relationship Assumptions 71

Chapter 5: Gaining Compassion for the Past 98

Chapter 6: Choosing Trust for the Future 113

Chapter 7: Practicing Stillness in the Present 139

Chapter 8: Obtaining Deliverance from Evil 159

Chapter 9: Letting God Love Us 186

Appendix 203

Acknowledgments 213

Notes 215

Index 219

INTRODUCTION

—◦❦◦—

When I was about five years old, someone gave me a small, iridescent butterfly pin with hinged wings that formed a tiny clasp. I loved how it held securely to my shirt so it would never get lost. I loved that even with my small fingers I could make its wings move, like the wings of a real butterfly. I still remember how much it delighted me.

One summer evening in the backyard, I started spinning in a circle with the butterfly in my outstretched hand, then releasing it into the air to let it fly. (And if you're having trouble getting into a story about a ceramic butterfly, think of it as a miniature stealth bomber with nuclear capability.) I then searched in the grass until I found the landing spot of the butterfly (or miniature stealth bomber with nuclear capability), secure in the assurance that toy butterflies do not really take flight, and that I was in control of this little portion of my world. I did this over and over with the delight only a five-year-old can find in such a simple game.

Then tragedy struck. I spun just as I always had, released the butterfly just as I always had, and searched just as I always had, but all I found in the grass was more grass. In violation of all my hard-won knowledge about the rules of How Things Work, the butterfly seemed to have truly taken flight. I searched for what seemed like forever, more and more frantic about my careless loss, but to no avail. I was devastated.

My mother, seeing my distress, offered, "Wendy, why don't we say a prayer. I'm sure Heavenly Father knows where the butterfly is." *Of course!* And so, I prayed. Then, full of faith, full of hope, I resumed my search. And in all the years we lived in that house, I never found the butterfly.

I learned early that prayer is not a magic wand we wave over the problems of our lives. It is not a bell we ring in a shop to let the owner know a customer is waiting. Genuine prayer involves more than performing a ritual, completing a duty, gaining public speaking skill, or learning some secret trick for getting our way. Prayer is how we express our love for God and invite His love to find us.

Prayer, then, is first and foremost a vehicle of relationship. When Alzheimer's disease robbed my mother of almost every capacity, including the ability to recognize her own children, some of her last comprehensible words were, "Heavenly Father, please help me." When my mother no longer knew my name, she knew God's, and she knew He knew her. Her relationship with Him was deep and instinctive, forged over a lifetime of seeking and listening to His voice.

When so much about finding the lost things we search for—whether things, or dreams, or help, or people—seems to hinge on the quality of our relationship with God, we would be foolish to give up on that relationship too quickly, even when it is hard, even when we aren't sure if God still knows our name, even when He doesn't come through for us as we think He should. As is the case with any mature relationship of genuine love, our relationship with God must accommodate both getting what we want and not getting it, times of closeness and times of distance, feeling fulfilled and feeling disappointed. God has to trust us to keep trusting Him even when He doesn't point out the location of all the things we pray to find. Betrayals we've experienced elsewhere can echo so loudly in our relationship with God that we end up covering our ears against Him, sometimes even without realizing we're doing it. We may even deliberately run from God, afraid of our clumsiness at love, or overwhelmed by the length of the journey from where we are to where He is, or mad enough to think we want the distance. Often we want to be found, but we aren't sure He's looking.

Our relationship with God, like any relationship, goes through stages and cycles of both closeness and distance, injury and repair. Heartaches, doubts, and trials do not affect us equally. Our stamina and skill for relating to God are impacted by how skilled we are at relationships in general, how tolerant we are of emotional intimacy, how humbly we can approach our weaknesses, how many different tools we've developed for connecting, how preoccupied we are with the often necessary busyness of life, how comfortable we've become with forgiving and being forgiven, and how deeply we've been hurt or betrayed in the past. There are many reasons we keep God at a distance, all the while thinking He is the one who chooses to stay away.

This Book

My hope in writing this book is to explore some of the reasons we keep God far away and how we might heal and hope enough to more fully receive the love He offers us. In it I draw primarily on my personal experience with this journey, but I am especially grateful for the many named (when I include a last name) and pseudonymed (when I don't) individuals who gave me permission to use their stories and perspectives. When I allude to God, I sometimes refer specifically to our Heavenly Father, to Jesus Christ, or to the Holy Ghost, but generally I assume that we build our relationship with all members of the Godhead in a similar fashion, united as They are, so I don't try to distinguish Them. Also, all italics in scriptural quotations are mine and are not in the original texts unless indicated.

In the first section of the book, we'll consider some of the ways our relationship with God may develop over time and see where we are on this journey. We'll look at assumptions we hold about human relationships in general that can interfere with our relationship with God, sometimes leaving us hesitant to commit to God or uncertain of how to receive His love. We'll also look at stages of long-term committed relationships and how they may apply to our relationship with God.

In the second section, we'll draw on lines from the Lord's Prayer that suggest opportunities for healing and deepening our relationship with God at any stage of our journey. We'll explore how our early family attachments may have either opened our hearts to connection with God or left us wary and overvigilant to danger. We'll look at the possible roles of anxiety, excessive busyness, temptation, and trauma in our relationship with God, and explore tools we can use now to be more open, present, and trusting.

Learning to let in the love God offers us seems to be the work of a lifetime. Although I have not found all my lost butterflies, I am increasingly in awe of God's kindness, patience, and willingness to come where I am, grieve with me for my losses, and encourage me to find my wings. I can honestly say these ideas have helped me deepen and broaden my relationship with God and find greater access to His constant companionship. I hope, indeed I pray, that they will be helpful to you.

Section One

THE JOURNEY OF RELATIONSHIP

Chapter 1

WHY IS GOD FAR AWAY?

—◦◦◦✦◦◦◦—

O God, where art thou? And where is the
pavilion that covereth thy hiding place?

(Doctrine and Covenants 121:1)

We learn who we are and what we can expect from others in the context of relationships. Some of what we learn from our mortal relationships encourages us to trust our Father in Heaven and His Son, Jesus Christ, and to reach optimistically toward Them. Some of what we learn can interfere with that trust, making it hard to comprehend Their love, let alone be filled with it. We can be left feeling dry and uprooted, unsure of how to tap into the living water at our feet.

It is difficult to grow a satisfying, trusting relationship with Divinity when prior relationship losses, disappointments, and fears entangle us in false hopes and impossible expectations. Why do our Father and Savior seem to stay so far away? Or are we putting up more obstacles to closeness than we realize? How can we learn to approach these—our most important relationships—with less worry and shame, more trust and hope? How can we more fully receive the love that we've been told They offer but that we don't always feel?

Without fully realizing it, many of us fear the vulnerability inherent in such closeness. We may yearn for an intimacy with God that we believe would quiet our fears, strengthen our confidence, and reassure our faith. But we are afraid of intimacy when we realize it would also expose our inadequacies or make us vulnerable to loss. We may have learned in relationships to feel overwhelmed, used, ignored, or afraid of betrayal, rejection, or disappointment. We may explicitly or implicitly worry that God will also criticize, ignore, deplete, or test us beyond our ability to endure.

Such fears may operate in the shadows, not drawing our attention. Then we look up one day from running our errands, calling the boss, watching the kids, and mowing the lawn to notice that something is off in our relationship with God. We're not even sure what. But it seems our fears have pushed our love for Him into the background, where it won't require so much of us or scare us so much. The results might look like this:

- "I don't feel like praying, and when I do, my prayers feel cool and I can't seem to connect. I even bore myself."
- "I know in my head that God is loving and kind, but my heart is afraid of His disappointment. I wonder if I can ever do enough to deserve His approval."
- "If God does all these miracles for others, why don't they happen to me? If He keeps others safe, why not me? If He heals others, why not me? If He sends angels to others, why not me? Why does God help me find my keys but not the things I need far more?"
- "I believe there is a God. He just doesn't seem to have a lot to do with my life right now."
- "I'm sure I could have been so much more faithful and effective if I had had more of the upbringing and opportunities others have had, or less of the disappointment and stress. It's

painful to realize I will never catch up. It doesn't seem fair that I'm so far behind."

+ "There hasn't been some huge falling out. I just don't feel as close as I'd like, and I'm not sure why."

Most of us have had at least fleeting thoughts of frustration or fear or confusion in our relationship with Deity. Often, we work it out. We change the way we think about things. We get another perspective or another calling. Something happens to comfort us or distract us. We move on.

Sometimes, however, the hard feelings do not dissipate or heal. They go underground, ready to re-emerge when we are over-stressed, tired, or confronted with some new temptation or challenge. Sometimes hard feelings become unwanted but familiar companions, far more willing to take a walk with us than God seems to be. We slip into their arms in search of some kind of justification for our doubts, some dark comfort for our wounds and fears. But we do not want to be here. We want to be in the loving embrace of our Father and our Savior. How do we end up instead in the unwelcome grasp of our shame, pride, fear, self-pity, boredom, or despair?

Faulty Assumptions, Not Just Faulty Behavior

While there may be multiple ways of understanding our relationship dilemmas with God (maybe we need clearer understanding of doctrine, more repentance, or greater patience), there is often something else at play that may not reflect a lack of righteousness on our part or a lack of accessibility on God's part. It may be simply that God is inviting us into a deeply intimate relationship with Him, and that this kind of closeness requires us to change not only our behavior but also some of our most basic assumptions about ourselves and life.

What kind of changes does such closeness require? The kind of change that occurs in a long and fruitful friendship or marriage as we learn to see ourselves—not just the other person—more clearly. The kind of change that requires us to repent and forgive. The kind of change that allows us to see our upbringing, weaknesses, and future with new eyes and broader perspective. The kind of change that comes from facing deep disappointment and finding a way to move forward with hope.

In other words, what has to change is not only our obvious sin, although that is also essential. What has to change may also be a conclusion we came to without knowing it was a conclusion, assuming instead that it was a fact about the world or ourselves, or a rule that would hold back trouble. A conclusion like: *People can't be trusted, and I'll be safe only if I'm always on guard.* But that conclusion no longer explains or protects. Now it holds us back and stops our relational growth.

What needs to change may be a familiar feeling or behavior that seems called for and even necessary to get us what we think we need. *If I take care of other people and never ask anything for myself, they will appreciate me and take care of me in return without me having to ask.* But acting this way leaves us with less instead of more.

What needs to change may be a rule we hold in our head about how other people are supposed to respond to us that gives us the illusion of control in an uncertain world. *If I let others know how accomplished (angry, scared, deserving, pained, funny) I am, they are supposed to let me have my way.* But illusions don't help us connect with the real God or the real world in a way that leads to trust and growth.

Other people may have told us our conclusion, feeling, behavior, rule, or illusion is hurting us more than it is helping. They counsel: *Stop worrying. Plan better. Try harder. Relax. Enjoy life. Get* to work. *Stand up for yourself. Stand back and let go. Stop fighting. Stop giving in.* We may try acting on their advice. The new approach may even work for a while, but then our worries turn out to be accurate, our losses real, our efforts useless, our positive thoughts pipe dreams. We end up feeling even more powerless, more exposed or betrayed. Or we may not have tried their advice because we can't even imagine what they are talking about, or can't imagine it working to save or solve or soothe.

We're stuck.

We don't know how to get around the unacceptable risks that genuine relationships impose, including the very real risk of getting hurt again, maybe—no, probably—in the exact same way we've been hurt before, and with the very hurt we were working so hard to avoid.

Spiritual maturity does not mean we've figured out how to not get hurt anymore, or how to not let pain get to us. Spiritual maturity includes:

- seeing choices we didn't realize we had, *including the choice to pick ourselves up and try again*
- asking humbly for what we need, and *tolerating the disappointment if we don't get it*
- praying with gratitude, repentance, and submission *more than with self-focused requests*
- sharing our thoughts or feelings *even when others disagree with us*
- listening with curiosity and empathy *even when we disagree with others*
- mourning when mourning is called for, and *letting others mourn with us*

- enduring uncertainty and suffering when required, *not assuming we must avoid them at all costs*
- learning from spiritual failure *without letting it define us*

Being a spiritual adult means being strong enough to tolerate being vulnerable. And being vulnerable is what many of us have learned, through a life full of vulnerability, to try to avoid at all costs.

Who Do I Think God Is?

I'm not nearly as spiritually mature as I'd like to be. I still carry around all sorts of unhelpful assumptions about relationships that sneak into my thinking, especially when I'm tired or overstressed. A few of these unhelpful assumptions are:

- People come in two flavors—needy and critical—and both types of people will eventually run over the top of me if I'm not careful.
- Appearing needy or vulnerable myself is extremely dangerous, and something others will criticize and look down on.
- Looking strong and in control, however, will only encourage others to expect too much from me.
- Letting people get too close is asking for trouble.

These assumptions not only get in the way of my relationships with people; they get in the way of my relationship with God. Mind you, I have a pretty clear understanding of who God tells us He is. I know He says He is loving and forgiving, generous and patient. But that belief doesn't always penetrate my soul. If I'm not very careful, I can assume without even realizing it that God also comes in two flavors: needy and critical. Either He will expect more from me than I can give, forever wheedling for more and more of my time, patience, money, or energy—or He will be critical and demanding, quick to point out my failures and denounce my flaws.

In my better moments I know it is time to lay those assumptions aside and trust more fully that God really is who He proclaims. And in my better moments I even succeed—for a time. But then God invites me to do something more when I'm already swamped, and I think, "See? He expects too much!" (as opposed to, "I can do this because He is going to help me"). Or He brings to my attention a flaw it is time to address, and I think, "See? He's always disappointed! And mean!" (as opposed to, "He loves me enough to help me see how to improve"). I assume I can never do enough to merit the protection, the approval, or the closeness I long for. I assume God keeps His distance because He is dissatisfied with me. I assume He is a mystery I can never solve. I don't always think like this, but the undercurrent of such assumptions pulls at me even when my more conscious thoughts toward God are grateful and adoring.

Getting Closer

My assumptions were challenged one day more than fifteen years ago in a completely unexpected way. My home office at that time had a large desk, two overstuffed chairs with an ottoman between them, and a large picture window overlooking a grove of trees. I was in the habit of sitting in one of the big chairs by the window to pray, looking at a spot in the sky above the trees as I presented my needs to God, up there in heaven. Petitional prayer, grateful prayer, even listening prayer came pretty naturally to me after years of practice. I had learned to speak freely to God of my desires for His blessings, my concerns for those I love, my struggles and gratitudes and hopes. But on that day I don't recall that I was particularly concerned about anyone, nor was I upset or worried.

I was simply gazing at the distant sky and talking to God as I often did about whatever was on my mind when a still, small voice startled me by talking back. Out of the blue (pretty literally), the question came clearly and distinctly into my mind:

Why do you keep me so far away?

The question stopped me cold—both because it wasn't often that I had such a direct experience of the Spirit speaking words to me, and because the question itself caught me completely off guard. Most of my life I have wanted—*longed*, in fact—to feel closer to God. I certainly never thought *I* was the one who kept *Him* at a distance. Not intentionally, and not consciously. I could feel my mind sort of grind to a stop; I was sputtering and stammering and blinking in confusion. I could not quite imagine what to think, but the implication of the question was clear: God was inviting me to invite Him closer. For right now, at least, I was in charge of the distance I felt between us.

I had had intimate experiences with God before, close and personal moments of sweet and pure revelation. But it had always felt like such moments were quite beyond my ability to ever control. In fact, the more I had insisted on answers, or clung to whatever voice might offer them, the more elusive both became.

But here was this question, hanging in the air, and there was God, somewhere up in the sky, waiting for my response.

Not sure what else to do, I took my eyes off the spot up there in the sky, turned my attention to the chair on the other side of the ottoman, and tried to imagine God there instead of up in the clouds. But the oddest thing happened: I just couldn't look. I wanted to disappear into the floor, the pillow, the blinds. I felt in some way I couldn't even fathom that God really came to that chair, and I couldn't meet His gaze. I began to weep uncontrollably. I had the strongest urge to fall down on the floor and sob at His feet. The words of Isaiah came forcefully and meaningfully to my memory and heart, and I understood them in some new place in my soul:

"Woe is me! for I am undone; because I am a man of unclean lips, and I dwell in the midst of a people of unclean lips: for mine eyes have seen the King, the Lord of hosts" (Isaiah 6:5).

Woe, woe indeed! It took several minutes and several attempts before I could so much as raise my face to imagine the face of God so, so close. I thought I would never stop crying, so deep was the reverence that I felt. At the same time, I've never felt more keenly the chasm between His goodness and my fallen-ness. Was it only minutes, or years, until my heart finally adjusted to this new proximity, like eyes adjusting to a bright, bright light? Ever so slowly I started to feel that perhaps I could tolerate this state of affairs enough to at least look at where God seemed to be.

And when I did, somewhere in my mind He spoke again. Sweetly. Gently. And yet His words pierced my soul:

Why do you keep me so far away?

My heart caught. But He was so close! So close that I almost couldn't breathe for the intensity of that nearness! Why would He want to be any closer to me, *me*, when He has so many billions of children to care for? I felt as if I could not tolerate being taken so seriously and known so intimately by the only, holy God. But the implications of the question were unmistakable. My weeping broke through again as I tried, almost painfully, to imagine Him yet closer, sitting on the ottoman only inches from my chair. Once again, I felt almost overcome, realizing that this new level of intimacy, though closer by only a few feet, was inexplicably different from the last. I had invited God into my room, but now I was allowing Him close enough to touch me with His finger. I felt as if His eyes, though unseen, penetrated my soul. Every instinct of my heart was to run and hide and beg Him not to look at me with such pure eyes. It was not that I felt displeasure or criticism or expectation from Him—not at all. It was just that I felt so known, more known than I have ever felt before. I could not hide. But hiding is what I do!

Nor could I hide from myself in the brightness of that gaze. It was not that I could not stand to see how bad I was. What I could not stand was to see how loved I was, how valued, how known. The very things I had longed for now seemed to burn me as I got so close to them. I sat folded up in my overstuffed chair, barely able to raise my eyes to consider the spot where I was now allowing God to be. Only slowly, gradually, did my crying slow as I opened my heart a little more to the overwhelming awe and reverence I felt for God. I realized with complete astonishment how utterly true it was that I was the one who had kept Him away, for I obviously could barely, *barely* tolerate what I was experiencing.

And then, as I felt myself begin to breathe again, I could sense He was about to speak again. I heard within my mind the question:

Why do you keep me so far away?

The question now felt truly unbearable. The only way God could come any closer would be for Him to put His arms around me, His face next to my face, His eyes too close to possibly evade. How, how could I let the God of heaven love me that much? How could I even permit myself to believe that the Creator of the universe would come to my little room and sit in my little chair and look into my little eyes and hold me in His holy, holy arms? And yet there He was, humbly waiting on my permission, my willingness to receive Him.

I let God hold me that day. With the eyes of my soul, I saw Him step out of His big world into my small world and embrace me with a love so knowing and so real that I have no words with which to describe it. The experience was neither coddling nor infantilizing, nor did I feel grand or important in the slightest. I have never felt so completely, or so humbly, myself. Whatever else that experience meant to me remains beyond my words to express.

I would have to say that I am still not sure what to make of that encounter. I don't know if I met up with some spiritual manifestation of God, or some representative, or a memory from eons gone by. It probably doesn't matter. On that day, I felt as if I were standing in a searing flame more real than anything else in the entire world.

Remarkably, regrettably, I still have to work very, very hard to let God close. I have never had an experience quite like that one again. I still struggle at times when I remember what that closeness felt like. It can still feel incomprehensibly difficult to open myself up to God.

So really—why *do* we keep God so far away?

Perhaps because we've learned through hard experience that relationships—even the ones we think we want—are dangerous. Fortunately, they are also the very best things in our lives.

Examining Our Relationship Assumptions

Some of my assumptions about relationships are like weeds that choke the tree of my faith, weeds I have not yet eradicated even though they need to die. Some days my fear of being overwhelmed by God, or becoming a religious fanatic, or not making the connection I long for means I avoid prayer completely. I don't recognize the problem for what it is. I think I just "forget." Or "get busy." More often I speak the words of prayer, but I am back to imagining God in some faraway place, and I don't fully understand why. I may believe that He hears my petitions, but I don't seem to find the door I need to open to let Him sup with me. Sometimes I can feel Him right there, waiting, near, my constant companion, but I don't know how to feel about it, or I can't quite receive what He offers.

Still, I am learning to once in a while tolerate intimacy, to be almost comfortable "encircled about eternally in the arms of his love" (2 Nephi 1:15). On at least some occasions I seem able to let myself believe that God wants to be as close to me as I will let Him. On those days, it is as if I take His arm as I face a difficult challenge. It is as if His hands rest on my head, blessing me when I am in need. It is as if the angel of His presence embraces me and whispers to me that He's *right here, right now.* And so am I: right here, right now, with Him.

It seems completely presumptuous to me to imagine that God loves me with what feels like the doting affection of a tender parent, the powerful love of a knowing father, but I try not to argue. I try to simply receive and to respond with my whole heart to the closeness that God seems to be offering. I have also had to learn that I do not control the distance between me and God—not completely. I cannot force this intimacy, and I cannot create it alone. Nor can I forget it—or the hope it engenders in my heart.

There are many kinds of prayer. There is the kind of prayer in which we ask God for things we need. There is the kind in which we rail about the things that stir us up, or list the blessings we hope He never yanks away. And then there is the kind of prayer in which the only object is to be close, to hold still in God's presence, to take in the reality that we are never out of it. In all kinds of prayer, I am trying to learn not to see God as a fickle parent whose moods I try to read so I can get permission to use the car. To no longer see prayer as a magic trick that if I could just get right (do long enough, in the right way, with the right words and attitudes) would produce the goodies or the goodness I long for. Sometimes God alone—His companionship, His perspectives, His love, His reminders—God alone becomes enough.

Changing Our Relationship Assumptions

Christ's disciples once asked Him to teach them to pray (see Luke 11:1). He can teach us, too. Sometimes we need more practice with submissive prayer, or grateful prayer, or penitent prayer. Sometimes we need to try praying longer, out loud, or with a paper and pencil in hand. And sometimes we need to simply invite God to join us at whatever empty chair we see or can imagine, opening our heart to let Him come close and sit with us as we wrestle with a problem, or feel sad, or just stare in wonder at the night sky.

We all have, by definition, a personal relationship with God, who is eternally our Father. But we must individually choose to foster and receive the covenant relationship that brings us back into His presence for eternity. I don't build a relationship with my husband by constantly asking him for favors, though I may ask him for favors. I don't build a relationship with my mother by only thanking her for her help, though I surely should thank her. I don't build a relationship with my friend by cajoling and pleading at every turn, though sometimes I may cajole and plead. I build relationships with people by sharing their company, walking with them in the park, laughing together, crying together, having long talks about nothing in particular, struggling together with a problem, feeling heard, sharing hugs, working side by side, hearing their stories, telling them mine, serving on their committees, sitting with them on the beach at sunset, learning from them, teaching them, and saying nothing at all. And when the chips are down, I build relationships with other people by sharing my most intimate fears and hurts, letting myself be cared for, apologizing, forgiving, seeing what really is, and not running. Such experiences teach me, also, how to have a personal relationship with God.

James G. Stokes, born with a condition that has required more than fifty surgical procedures in his twenty-eight years of life, faced yet another long hospitalization. He writes:

> . . . on what felt like the darkest and most dismal night I had ever faced, I forgot the many blessings I had received from the Lord. I thought only of the sorry state of my life. My negativity engulfed me, and I began to doubt all I had been taught about my Heavenly Father and His Son, Jesus Christ. A loving God, I rationalized, would not have left me alone to face this nightmarish reality. . . .
>
> I was about to voice these thoughts in prayer when I heard my name. Through my anguish I recognized the voice of the Spirit, carrying a message to my soul from my Savior reminding me I was not alone. Jesus Christ knew what I was going through. He had felt my pain. . . .
>
> This reminder forever changed the way I look at the Atonement of Jesus Christ.[1]

I believe that God loves us with—dare I say it?—with a daddy's love, a mama's love. Not the daddy or the mama we had, but the one we need now. Even when others cannot fully grasp our feelings, He can, and He does. That is not to say that I believe He wants us to be like little children sitting on His knee. But it is to say that I believe His love for us is passionate and consuming and personal. He knows us by name. He has, in fact, named us, and named us with the names of His power. He wants to teach us who He is as well, to reveal to us His identity as a healer, a life giver, an empowerer, an embracer, a teacher, a redeemer, a friend. In such proximity to God we learn most fully who we are.

I also believe it grieves God when we keep Him far away (see Moses 7:31–33). Sometimes when we are pounding and pounding on the door, hoping beyond hope that He is standing on the other side and will open to us if we pound long enough or hard enough or with just the right rhythm or intensity or insistence, sometimes at just those moments we need to stop pounding and take another look. The door to the soul opens in (see Revelation 3:20).

Opening the Door

The first commandment we are given as new members of the Church is to "receive the Holy Ghost." We are also invited to receive commandments, messengers, grace, spiritual gifts, priesthood power, hope, forgiveness, baptism, the gospel, strength, evidences, testimony, revelation, blessings, our bodies, other people, exaltation . . . and God. Opening our hearts to receive is our responsibility and privilege. Let's try a little exercise to illustrate this:

1. Hold out your hand. Please? Just for a moment.
2. What does it look like? Is it poised to receive?

Try out some of the different ways we might hold our hand out to another:

+ Make a fist. If we feel vulnerable or exposed, we may prepare to fight or grasp and cling instead of opening ourselves up to receive.
+ Hold up a "stop" hand. If we feel skeptical or resistant we may push others away instead of bring them closer.
+ Open your palm, fingers flat. If we feel distrustful or resistant we may let everything run through our fingers to show that nothing can affect us, or to make clear that we never get enough.

+ Reach out to shake hands. If we desire connection and co-operation we may offer them, wondering what will happen when we do.
+ Cup your hand. If we are hopeful and trusting we may shape our hand to make a receiving place that we trust can be filled as often as we need.

When you think about your *current* relationship with God, how would you hold your hand to reflect it?

How would you like to be? Hold your hand in a way that would capture that. Notice how it feels. Let your heart soften just a little into that posture.

Remembering

Jesus taught His disciples to pray both through direct instruction and by example. Perhaps the most poignant of His prayers was offered in Gethsemane, where Jesus atoned for the sins of the world. We have only the briefest record of that prayer, but in it we learn about a kind of relationship with God that is so personal, so tender, that we, with the Apostles, almost feel we have to close our eyes against its intimacy. Jesus requests: "Abba, Father, all things are possible unto thee; take away this cup from me: nevertheless not what I will, but what thou wilt" (Mark 14:36).

Abba—the most familiar, familial, intimate name for Father. Our modern equivalent would be Papa. Dad. This appellation contrasts with His plea from the cross, "My God, my God, why hast thou forsaken me?" (Mark 15:34). In Gethsemane, although He has taught His disciples that God knows how to give good gifts to His children and will not, if they ask for bread or fish, give them a stone or a serpent (see Luke 11:11–13), Jesus's petition for the removal of the bitter cup is not granted. On Calvary, His question about God's apparent absence goes unanswered. The hard stone of

Gethsemane is what He gets—not bread. The serpent's handiwork is everywhere.

There *is* a response to Christ's prayer in Gethsemane, however. Although He must drink the foreordained cup, a heavenly companion comes to mourn with Him: "there appeared an angel unto him from heaven, strengthening him" (Luke 22:43). Ultimately, whatever the immovable stone or the fiery serpent we face, the companionship of heaven is our greatest need as well. And just as Christ must remember on the cross that God is His Father, even when He seems far away, so we must remember in *our* dark hours the companionship of heaven we have once experienced, even if we do not experience it now. Though His plea on the cross about being forsaken is the only prayer Christ addresses to "God" and not "Father," Christ acknowledges again His trust in God as His Father with His final prayer of complete submission: "Father, into thy hands I commend my spirit" (Luke 23:46).

Gethsemane required Jesus to accept the strengthening hand of a messenger—instead of the escape He had prayed for. Calvary required Jesus to hold fast to what He knew about His Father's love—even when His Father seemed far away. Such prayers are less about trying to make sure God knows us and our needs, and more about receiving and remembering what He has already given.

Such prayers can be especially difficult when our earthly experiences have taught us to fear abandonment or rejection. It is a rare person whose relationships have been so consistently trustworthy as to not instill at least a few such fears.

Father

The name of Jehovah was not spoken by the Jews because it was considered too sacred to utter. Yet God seems to be forever inviting us to call out His name, open our hearts to His companionship,

learn about His character and identity, and make that character
and identity our own.

Elder Bruce R. McConkie taught:

> We don't need to think everlastingly about God our
> Eternal Father as being an omnipotent, almighty, glori-
> fied person. . . . We might do better to think of God our
> Father as just that—as a father . . . as a personal being
> whose face we have seen and in whose household we have
> dwelt, whose voice we have heard, whose teachings we have
> learned before ever we were born into this life.[2]

President Boyd K. Packer spoke in a similar vein:

> For now I offer this comfort: God is our Father! All
> the love and generosity manifest in the ideal earthly father
> is magnified in Him who is our Father and our God be-
> yond the capacity of the mortal mind to comprehend.[3]

Paul adds another apostolic witness of this sacred truth:

> For as many as are led by the Spirit of God, they are
> the sons [and daughters] of God.
>
> For ye have not received the spirit of bondage again to
> fear; but ye have received the Spirit of adoption, whereby
> we cry, Abba, Father.
>
> The Spirit itself beareth witness with our spirit, that
> we are the children of God:
>
> And if children, then heirs; heirs of God, and joint-
> heirs with Christ. . . .
>
> For I am persuaded, that neither death, nor life, nor
> angels, nor principalities, nor powers, nor things present,
> nor things to come,
>
> Nor height, nor depth, nor any other creature, shall be

able to separate us from the love of God, which is in Christ Jesus our Lord. (Romans 8:14–17, 38–39)

We can choose, heal, and deepen our relationship with God our Father and His Son, Jesus Christ. We do this more readily as we better understand the impact of our mortal relationships on our assumptions about love, as we change our minds about the fears our relationships have taught us to harbor, and as we repent, forgive, work, and receive so God can meet our truest needs. We may still have to make do with something other than the relief we seek. We may still feel at times that God has forsaken us. We may still have to choose to remember and trust what we cannot now feel or see. But I believe it is also still true that God is closer to us than we know, and wants to be closer still.

Chapter 2

STAGES OF COMMITTED
RELATIONSHIPS

—⟨∘⟩✠⟨∘⟩—

The Lord hath redeemed my soul . . . and I
am encircled about eternally in the arms of his love.
(2 Nephi 1:15)

The scriptures use many metaphors to describe our relationship with God. In the Old Testament, Isaiah says, "But now, O Lord, thou art our father; we are the clay, and thou our potter; and we all are the work of thy hand" (Isaiah 64:8; see also Jeremiah 18:2–6). God is the Artist who creates out of a lifeless lump whatever He desires. Through the course of our relationship with Him, we can expect to be molded into something beautiful.

In the New Testament, the Savior teaches, "I am the vine, ye are the branches: He that abideth in me, and I in him, the same bringeth forth much fruit: for without me ye can do nothing" (John 15:5), and in the Book of Mormon Jacob compares God to a gardener for whom we are the plants (see Jacob 5:41, 47). In these scriptures we move up in the world from a lump of clay to a living thing. Through our connection with God we can expect both to be nourished and to become fruitful. Without it, we die.

Jesus tells the New Testament Saints, "I am the good shepherd: the good shepherd giveth his life for the sheep" (John 10:11). With this analogy we join the animal kingdom, and Christ herds, feeds, and protects us as His sheep. We can expect as a result of our relationship with Him to be cared for and sacrificed for. Without it, we become the prey of the predator of our soul.

In Leviticus 25:55, Jehovah compares us to slaves whom He has purchased for Himself and freed from the taskmasters of Egypt: "For unto me the children of Israel are servants; they are my servants whom I brought forth out of the land of Egypt: I am the Lord your God." In our relationship with God we can expect to work hard, owing our lives to our Master who has bought us out of the slavery of infinitely less fair or charitable circumstances.

In Galatians 4:6–7, Paul brings us into an even higher status when he teaches, "And because ye are sons, God hath sent forth the Spirit of his Son into your hearts, crying, Abba, Father. Wherefore thou art no more a servant, but a son; and if a son, then an heir of God through Christ." Here our relationship with God is a familial bond in which we can expect to be taught, to be cherished, and to be heirs of all the Father has. We are, in the words of a sweet hymn by Isaac Watts, "no more a stranger, nor a guest, but like a child at home."[1]

All of these analogies teach us something important about our relationship with God, the reverence we owe Him, the superiority of His wisdom and power over our own, and even the benevolent, self-sacrificing devotion with which He regards us. But in the book of Hosea, God ups the ante even further. Hosea is a prophet at a time when Israel is estranged from God, and God is trying to call her back into her covenant bond with Him. Hosea quotes God as saying so poetically about Israel:

> Therefore, behold, I will allure her, and bring her into the wilderness, and speak comfortably unto her.
> And I will give her her vineyards from thence, and the

valley of Achor for a door of hope: and she shall sing there, as in the days of her youth, and as in the day when she came up out of the land of Egypt.

And it shall be at that day, saith the Lord, that thou shalt call me Ishi; and shalt call me no more Baali. (Hosea 2:14–16)

What do these titles mean? *Baali* means "master" or "lord," a fitting designation for Israel to use with her God, but Jehovah says it is not the title He wants with them ("call me no more Baali"). Instead He desires the title of *Ishi*: "husband."

God is inviting His chosen Israel to be not just pots or plants or sheep or slaves or even children and heirs in His household, but to be as a married wife to Him, as a chosen spouse who calls Him husband. He adds:

And I will betroth thee unto me for ever; yea, I will betroth thee unto me in righteousness, and in judgment, and in lovingkindness, and in mercies.

I will even betroth thee unto me in faithfulness: and thou shalt know the Lord. (Hosea 2:19–20)

I don't claim to fully grasp what the Lord is offering us in these and other similar verses (see, for example, Isaiah 54:5; Revelation 19:7). At minimum, perhaps God is implying that what it takes to have a good relationship with Him is at least something like what it takes to have a good marriage with a fellow mortal: faithfulness, loving kindness, forgiving, deeply knowing, and being deeply known. He seems to be inviting us to *that* kind of intimacy and oneness—an invitation that would be completely preposterous to contemplate were it not that God Himself has proposed it to us.

A loving marriage is a uniquely intimate bond. Within marriage, most of us hope to be known and accepted for who we are and to be encouraged and supported in our growth. We hope to be with someone we respect and desire who respects and desires us in return. This level of unity and connection does not occur overnight. It requires taking the incredible risk of falling in love with someone who, in the big scheme of things, we barely know, committing our lives to another despite being more different than we now imagine. It requires learning to see what is wrong with us when we prefer to see what is wrong with our spouse. It requires tolerating distance and loss without giving up on the promises of a shared eternity. It requires accepting our spouse and ourselves at a deeper level than we can at first imagine, encircling our differences with a genuine compassion that negates shame and empowers trust.

How do we build such a bond—a relationship worth perpetuating for eternity? How do we build it with people? How do we build it with God?

Stages of Long-Term Committed Relationships

If God is proposing to us, offering to be our husband, our intimate partner, then learning about what makes other long-term committed relationships work may be our best guide for helping us connect deeply with God.

People have done a lot of contemplation and research about how marriages unfold, and many of them note that loving, successful marriages often evolve in predictable stages.[2] These stages seem to apply to other close, long-term relationships as well. You may or may not recognize these stages in your relationships, but if you do, you are certainly not alone. Even if your relationships do not rigidly follow these stages, you may notice elements of them showing up from time to time. When they do, we get to work at increasing our relationship skills, healing our relationship wounds, and defusing our relationship land mines. God can use any and all of our human relationships and experiences to teach us what we personally came here to learn and to help us grow in our relationship with Him.

However (and this is a big *however*), if you are in a troubled marriage, or if you're divorced, or if you have never married (or maybe don't even want to), what follows could be a little distracting. It may help to think about another type of relationship, like a parent-child relationship, a deep friendship, or even something like a mission or a career, as I explain these stages. But since these stages were first observed in marriage, and since God compares your relationship with Him to a loving marriage, I hope you'll keep reading, even if you have to stretch a bit to imagine these stages having anything to do with your life. Then we'll talk specifically about how these stages can apply to a personal relationship with God.

Stage One: The Honeymoon

For many people, the first stage of a long-term committed relationship is the Honeymoon Stage. Compared to later stages of a marriage, this early stage of falling in love, committing to each other, and enjoying the public celebration of becoming a family together is especially idealistic and delightful. We may think with wonder and joy, "Somebody loves me and chooses me—somebody whom I also love and choose!" There is often a sense at this stage that we *get* each other, that our bond is a special one that won't erode. Although we recognize that marriage is a bit of a gamble, we also tend to believe we're different from other couples. We may assume *we* will always work things out because, unlike others, *we* know how to really communicate! *We're* so much alike in the things that really matter! *We're* going to build a wonderful life!

President Boyd K. Packer described this stage beautifully as follows:

Ideally, mating begins with romance. Though customs may vary, it flourishes with all the storybook feelings of excitement and anticipation, even sometimes rejection. There are moonlight and roses, love letters, love songs, poetry, the holding of hands, and other expressions of affection between a young man and a young woman. The world disappears around the couple, and they experience feelings of joy.[3]

As we build our dreams for the future, we may have wonderful moments of delight, passion, and deepening and wondrous affection. Not only do we get to feel cherished and desired, but we often feel magically charitable, kind, and selfless in turn. It can feel miraculously easy to be good when we have just the right partner to inspire our best self. This stage of marriage builds a foundation of mutual delight and desire. In other relationships, it may feel like we've been given the one perfect baby, or we've been called to the perfect mission for us, or we've finally found the ideal career. Hallelujah!

This stage can also propel us into a fantasy world in which we expect the other person to understand us fully and we expect to fully understand him or her. We think this child will turn out much like us, only better, or that this mission or career will capitalize on our strengths and negate our weaknesses. We may assume that within this ultimate mutual acceptance our unseen wounds will heal and our potential will be released. We may expect life to get much easier now that we have finally found the person (or calling, or friendship) with whom we are so deeply compatible.

Whatever our experience is with falling in love and making a commitment, the Honeymoon Stage doesn't last forever, however. In fact, many marriage researchers conclude that marriage partners not only are not fully compatible in the ways they may imagine when they fall in love, but that we generally choose marriage partners with whom we are *inherently and specifically incompatible.*[4] So within a few years, or months, or sometimes even hours of say- ing "I do," this stage generally gives way to . . .

Stage Two: Power Struggle

Suddenly or gradually, we realize the person we married isn't just the wonderful life partner of our dreams. He or she is also fundamentally different from us, and our life together may be quite different from what we thought we signed up for. In fact, at times we may wonder if we even know who this person is at all. We may think, "He not only doesn't completely and fully understand me, he doesn't even understand the most important and basic things about me." "She doesn't share all my goals, dreams, feelings, opin- ions, and routines—in fact, she doesn't even share my most ba- sic assumptions about who is supposed to do what laundry, how money should be spent, the role of sex in a marriage, or how chil- dren or in-laws should be dealt with." In this stage, the people on our mission all seem to hate us, and the food is awful. The baby has colic. The friend turns just plain weird. The teenager is a complete enigma.

Fortunately, we often sort things out. Someone apologizes, someone else accepts, we get through a problem—and we feel better afterwards, more committed, and relieved to find out we married a reasonable person after all, or moved into the right ward, or bought the right house. But then the problem returns or a new one devel- ops, and we may once again wonder how it all got so complicated. Even when we find someone as much like us as we possibly can, there are often enough differences to drive us both crazy at times.

A value of this stage of marriage is the introduction of realism and the push to grow. The goal of the gospel is not to make us all so alike that we can finally get along, but to teach us the curiosity, open-mindedness, discernment, and compassion to love what we would otherwise be incapable of loving. Every dream comes with its share of challenges, and the very specific unexpectedness of those challenges is part of what makes them so hard.

One marital researcher notes that the marital problems of the couples he studies fall into two categories—problems they can solve and problems they can't solve. At the Power Struggle Stage, we assume the problems we struggle with are solvable, if we can learn the right way to talk, the right way to listen, the right way to negotiate, or the right way to influence. We have at least some confidence that these are normal problems we will get through, restoring us to the contentment and bliss of the Honeymoon Stage. But what percent of the problems in successful marriages are solvable problems that people actually work through? Among the long-term, successful marriages studied by this leading marital researcher, the percentage of problems that actually got fully resolved was 31 percent. That means 69 percent of marital problems were never fully solved.[5]

You read that right. Even in good marriages, couples who come to a research laboratory to talk about a problem will, when they come back years later, still stew about the same problem 69 percent of the time. These problems are like a trick knee or chronic asthma—ailments that come and go in importance but don't just go away altogether. We simply learn to cope with them as best we can, or work around them, or lessen their intensity, or ignore them.

What does this look like with a marital "chronic illness"? It means uniting with our spouse against the problem instead of making each other into the problem. It means we listen, share, and try again. It means we try to keep a sense of humor, get some counseling, read a book, or make a chore chart. With other people or in other situations it may mean we keep working anyway, remember the alternatives might actually be worse, do our homework, take a parenting class, or talk to our mission president. And if those things don't always work as well as we'd like, we may next go through . . .

Stage Three: Withdrawal

In this stage of a long-term committed relationship, we may feel like we've done all we can to work things out and we just can't take it anymore. We aren't necessarily leaving, although this stage is the most dangerous one for marriages. But we may increasingly conclude that we've tried everything we can think of and nothing works, or that we are both just too busy or disenchanted to do the work that relationships seem to require. We may increasingly go our own way and do our own thing and let our spouse do the same. We may stay for the kids or our parents or the money. We may stay because we don't want the stigma of divorce or coming home early from the mission or quitting the job. We may stay because we can't really imagine starting over, because we get along well enough for now, or because we just don't let ourselves think about the alternative. But we may not necessarily be happy about it. And we may not be hopeful about it.

Counseling, praying together, going on more dates, serving the other, or trying yet again to talk through a tough issue can all be helpful. But they don't magically change our partner back into the loving, generous, delightful person we thought we married. And they don't magically change us back into that loving, generous, delightful person we so easily were in the Honeymoon Stage.

What may change, however, is our self-awareness. We may start challenging ourselves to be more accepting, forgiving, understanding, apologetic, independent, or engaged. We may begin to realize just how annoying we are, how much our spouse or companion or teenager has to put up with. And in that process of personal growth, something about our expectations of marriage or life also begins to shift. We may look around and realize we have it better than our friend or our brother. We may notice that the kids like our spouse okay, so maybe we can too; or they don't, so maybe we'd better. We may begin to see our spouse with new appreciation for the unique, wounded, strong, weak, precious human being he or she is. Beginning with underwhelming declarations of renewed affection, we may gradually decide to like each other again, or more, or differently. We may remember the reasons we fell in love, even if they don't all hold in the same way. We may begin to deeply understand that God truly loves us both. We tiptoe into . . .

Stage Four: Acceptance and Renewal

Stage Four is when our dream of discovering (or being) a perfect spouse finally dies, and our goal of creating a marriage worth perpetuating for eternity comes alive. We can come to a place of deeper acceptance of our spouse as a real human being whose dreams, heartaches, and fears matter to us and whose underlying goodness we cherish. Not everyone will reach this stage in this life or stay in it permanently once we do, but as we approach this stage we begin to see our spouse much more clearly for who he or she is: different from us and from who we first thought, wished, or needed him or her to be—but someone we choose, despite these differences, to trust, to love, and to like. The problems may not all get solved, but we learn to work around them, to keep our sense of humor, to see our point of view as just another point of view instead of the one and only right and true way to do life. We are humbled by our partner's deep virtues, deep hurts, and deep preciousness to the Lord. We see ourselves as fallible and faulty contributors to our marital challenges, and we want to try harder. We choose to be more humble, more patient, kinder, gentler. We are deeply grateful for the acceptance our spouse offers, or for the ways he or she has helped us be better. We see the fear under the anger, the hurt under the fear. We make peace with where we are as a couple. We don't stop growing, but we also realize that what we have already is good—and enough for now. We have done the hard work of being vulnerable in a real relationship, and we are finding a true home in each other.

President Boyd K. Packer summarizes our marital journey and its possibilities:

> If you suppose that the full-blown rapture of young romantic love is the sum total of the possibilities which spring from the fountains of life, you have not yet lived to see the devotion and the comfort of longtime married love. Married couples are tried by temptation, misunderstandings, financial problems, family crises, and illness, and all the while love grows stronger. Mature love has a bliss not even imagined by newlyweds.[6]

Marriage is a lifelong, even eternal commitment to someone with whom we may be far less compatible than we initially assume. As we learn to respond to these surprises with intentionality and charity instead of demand and disappointment, we participate in an amazing school that can help us to heal even if we aren't cured, to find strength even though we are weak, and to gain the immense spiritual power of godly compassion. We not only learn to love this person who is so unlike us, but in the process we also learn to accept and heal the outcasts within our own psyche that we have also wanted to reject. We stop waiting for someone else to provide the magic, healing acceptance we yearn for; instead, we claim that healing acceptance from God and from ourselves.

We don't get to this final stage of deep commitment, eyes-open love, healing, and growth by jumping ship and starting over with someone else in the Honeymoon Stage because the Honeymoon Stage doesn't last forever, for anyone, nor should it. The Honeymoon Stage is like the Garden of Eden to which cherubim and a flaming sword keep us from returning, not because God is mean or our failures are too astronomical to go unpunished, but because the only way to get where we ultimately desire to be is to go forward, not back. Our journey through the power struggles and lonely isolation of a dreary world can eventually bring us to cherish and receive the reconciliation of the Atonement, the At-one-ment, all the while teaching us to be more like God: more humble, more empathetic, more trustworthy, more redemptive, more creative, more present, more real.

How This Helps

Learning about these stages has helped me see a bigger picture of where my relationships have been, where they generally are now, and where they might yet go. I can also see how my relationships cycle among these stages in the short term, bouncing around among them on any given issue. I feel less stupid and stuck, and clearer about what I personally could work on to improve, when I can see the lay of the land.

Of course, when we are in the Honeymoon Stage, this all sounds like nonsense. I still remember teaching these ideas to a class of BYU students and seeing the skeptical, unhappy looks on their faces as I intimated that maybe they were in for a wild ride. One student, newly married, came back to class the next week and raised her hand. She wanted to make it clear that she had not believed a word of the information I had charted out the previous week. She was convinced that she and her husband would never go through these stages because of their superior compatibility, communication skills, commitment to each other and God, and amazing family role models. In fact, she had told her mother about what I'd taught—her mother whose marriage this student deeply admired—and then had asked her mother, "Mom, this teacher's wrong, isn't she? It doesn't have to be like this, right?" She was pretty startled when her mother replied, "Well, honey, it's not as bad as it sounds." That was *not* the reassuring answer she was looking for!

While learning about the stages of long-term committed relationships may not be terribly comforting when we are just starting out on the intimidating journey of creating an eternal family, beginning a mission, or choosing a career, it is *very* comforting if we get past the honeymoon and into a power struggle and wonder if we've made some horrible mistake. It really helps to know that the problems we experience are in fact common, and that a deeper but more realistic commitment and delight than we can now imagine might actually lie at the end of this bumpy road.

As noted, these four stages could apply in many settings—with a spouse, parents, children, a career, a mission, the Church, and Church leaders. We can use any of these types of long-term committed relationships to learn skills we can apply to any of the others, including to our relationship with God. Especially with God. Our *Ishi*. Our spouse. Because God is inviting us into a close, intimate, enduring, covenant relationship that may be more like a marriage than any of the other comparisons God uses to describe how we relate to Him.

Again, while we may not all recognize our relationships in all of these stages, we may go through them in a different order, or we may bounce around among them, let's now consider what these four stages might look like in our relationship with Deity.

The Honeymoon Stage with God

I affectionately think of the Honeymoon Stage of our spiritual life as the "girls' camp stage." We see in this stage the tender enthusiasm of a testimony meeting at the end of a Young Women camp, a new convert getting first answers to prayers, a new missionary discovering the joy of teaching the gospel, or a teenager feeling the Spirit confirm that the Book of Mormon is true. This can be an exuberant, dizzying stage of realizing that we can feel the Spirit for ourselves, that the doctrines of the Church resonate deeply with our soul, that a Church leader really is inspired, or that God really does offer us revelation. We might say with amazement, "I get this! I felt that! This is real! That is awesome! God's amazing! Why doesn't everyone see this?"

This stage of our spiritual lives is usually sweet and precious— the beginning of our commitment to God. We see a dramatic example of this stage in Joseph Smith's first prayer and vision. He writes of this experience, "and my soul was filled with love and for many days I could rejoice with great Joy and the Lord was with me."[7] Being filled with *love* and *joy* surely sounds like a honeymoon to me.

As in a marriage, this stage is often marked by public declarations of our commitment as we are baptized, bear our testimony, serve a mission, attend the temple, or in other ways make and express our covenant with God. We may have powerful spiritual experiences we will remember for the rest of our lives. Of course, we may also have periods of doubt or uncertainty that must be worked through, just as with a potential spouse, but we *do* work through them, for the most part at least, and as we do, we feel our commitment grow.

Some members can't remember when they didn't believe; they have a slowly simmering faith rather than one that came to a quick boil. They marry their high school sweetheart, so to speak. But when we claim the gospel and the Church as ours, acknowledge the reality of spiritual feelings and experiences, accept that God is real and Jesus is our Savior, and covenant to organize our lives around these truths, we enter our personal Honeymoon Stage with God or the Church (and those two things may be different). Months, years, even decades may unfold while we stay more or less in this stage. But then, gradually or suddenly, things may not only feel more difficult, they may feel that way a lot. We may find ourselves in . . .

The Power Struggle Stage with God

Just as no deep and committed adult relationship proceeds seamlessly, without a single disagreement, bringing our will into perfect alignment with God's will usually takes time, effort, self-reflection, and repentance. When problems develop that don't just go away on our timetable, it is good to remember that such challenges are common, even though often invisible to outsiders. If an esteemed bishop betrays our trust, a beloved family matriarch gets cancer and is not healed despite blessings that seem to promise healing, or questions come up that we can't find satisfactory answers to, our honeymoon feelings may suddenly feel like a thing of the past.

Sometimes we work out such challenges, and things settle down again. But sometimes the problem comes back with a new twist, or another one develops. We've come into faith with a sieve full of rocks and dirt that we keep shaking, and the little stuff all falls through, giving us hope that the rest will too. But after a while, we may be left with the boulders.

We may find ourselves thinking, "If God were really loving, He wouldn't act like this. If the Church is true, then its leaders shouldn't think like that. If the gospel is real, then I should be spared this loss, given this answer, provided this miracle. I can't do all this stuff God expects, and He doesn't seem to be helping. There shouldn't be injustice or wacko people in the Church. I shouldn't feel the same goose bumps in a testimony meeting that I feel at a Disney World parade."

Or we may find ourselves thinking, "I need to pray more, be better, have more faith. Once God sees my point of view on this, He will come through on His promises. There must be a way to get an education, have children, not go into debt, fulfill a Church calling, pay tithing, be a great parent, attend the temple every week, share the gospel with my neighbors, be active in community politics, and always be cheerful—or the talks at general conference wouldn't keep talking about them all. I'll figure it out eventually. I just need to try harder. And learn how to live without sleep."

As in a marriage or other long-term committed relationship, a high percentage of problems may simply not be fully resolvable in this life. But that doesn't mean we picked the wrong God or the wrong church. It does mean we may need a different strategy, greater patience, a sense of humor, more help, reminders of what we love about God or the Church, or more humble prioritization. It may also mean that some things about us, God, the gospel, and life really will not be the way we once imagined. We really cannot have it all. Life has always required us to choose, not just between good and evil but between good and better.

We might characterize Joseph Smith's struggle to get God to let him give Martin Harris the 116 pages of the Book of Mormon transcript as an example of a power struggle with God (see Doctrine and Covenants 3). Joseph gets answers, but they are answers he doesn't like, so he keeps pushing for different ones. He wants to do God's will, but he also wants Martin Harris to like him, God to protect him, and people to believe him. Finally, God lets him have his way, and the consequences follow: the pages are permanently lost and all that work of translation is for naught. Joseph learns the hard way that God knows more than he does, that he can't have it all, and that even though God can redeem anything He allows to happen to us, the things we need redemption from can really, really hurt. Yes, God loves us and will forgive us. But the cliffs we fall off when we ignore His warnings are real.

Ironically, God's rebuke of Joseph is the first revelation Joseph Smith records for inclusion in the public records of the Church. Joseph Smith seems to think the lessons he learned through his struggle are not for his benefit alone, but something of potential benefit to anyone in a power struggle with God. I'm so grateful for Joseph's willingness to be honest, vulnerable, and humble about his weaknesses and sins as he shares the story of his developing and powerful relationship with God.

Our personal power struggles with God may get triggered by conflict with a Church leader, frustration with a calling, dissatisfaction with our life circumstances, trouble with family members, disillusionment over some aspect of Church history or doctrine, discomfort with the temple, a personal weakness or sin, a promise that has not been fulfilled, or many other things. But just as we can't expect to simply change a spouse's personality or behavior, we can't change the Lord. To successfully navigate the power struggle, we have to open ourselves to the possibility that something *in us* needs changing instead.

That is not necessarily what we thought we signed up for. We thought we signed up for ministering angels, personal revelation, faith-promoting answers to prayers, and warm, happy feelings. So periods of power struggle can throw us for a loop. After months or years or decades of not getting all the answers we want and *need*, we may move into . . .

The Withdrawal Stage with God

Like those who turned away from the Savior when they could not understand Him (see John 6:66), there may be times when we feel like turning away from God. We may think, "I can't figure this out. I need a little distance here." Or, "Maybe I've taken this whole thing too seriously. Maybe I need a break. Maybe I should move to a new ward. Maybe I should be a Buddhist." Or, "People must not be thinking clearly if they don't have a problem with this. This is nuts. I just don't belong here. In fact, I'm not sure I ever did. I'm getting absolutely no help from God. Where did He go?" Or simply, "This is too hard. I don't know what to do. I'm not sure I'm ready to leave. But how much longer can I wait for answers that don't come?" Greg describes such a period in his life:

> My wife and I struggled with infertility for years. A few years ago we decided to pursue adoption. We tried so hard to follow the Spirit precisely through the entire process. After a year of our profile being online, we finally had a prospective mother contact us. This was a first for us, and a very exciting time. After much prayer and contemplation, we felt like God had other plans for us, however. We told her the news, never to hear from her again.
>
> The moment we sent the email, we felt horrible. Although we thought it was the right thing to do, everything started going wrong after that decision. We no longer felt the Spirit in our lives. We could not feel God's love. We questioned whether He was really there, or whether the church that we grew up in was true or not. We fasted, prayed, went to the temple, and improved ourselves the best we knew how, but we were unable to feel the Spirit in our lives for nearly two years. This was especially difficult as we had many important decisions to make about infertility treatments, other

adoption possibilities, and so many things. It felt like we were being punished for obeying God. We had never experienced that before. We believed that if you sought the Spirit and followed God's will, He'd support you in seeing it through. Instead, we felt like we followed Him and He yanked the rug out from under us. We KNEW logically that none of that was true, but it sure felt like it.

We learned that He's not always "there" when you need Him. He's often there, and he often answers right when we need it—we have lots of evidence and testimony of this. However, there are also times in our lives where He isn't there when we need Him (or at least when we *think* we need Him). . . . Even though they followed Moses and followed God, things got worse and worse for the children of Israel—right up to the moment when the Red Sea parted.

As I look back on that two years, I am so grateful for the family and teachers who had helped me develop this storehouse of faith, sort of like food storage, that I had to live on for a long time. Sometimes I wondered if it would hold out long enough. But I think people on both sides of the veil help us through our trials. The Spirit is starting to come back and show up again in my life, and I'm so grateful—grateful that I had enough "faith storage" to see me through those lean years.[8]

When we drove our college kids from Michigan to BYU in Utah, the longest part of the journey was Nebraska. The road through Nebraska was boring, flat, and everlasting. The Withdrawal Stage with God reminds me of Nebraska. My husband and I once had an amazing spiritual experience in Nebraska, and I've learned that there are parts of Nebraska that are delightful, but when we were just driving through, Nebraska wasn't even worth being awake for. Even the power struggle of Chicago rush hour was better than the long, dry trek through Nebraska. But there was no avoiding Nebraska if we wanted to get to "Zion."

In a similar way, many of us get to the culminating stage of acceptance and renewal with God only if we are willing to endure things we don't understand, prayers that aren't answered as we'd like, or challenges we hate. Intimacy with God is not just found in the intensity of honeymoons and power struggles; sometimes the only way we can prepare for new levels of intimacy is by just driving down that long, empty road.

On our road trips, distracting ourselves, playing games in our heads, taking breaks, and steady persistence all had their place. After a while we learned to actually enjoy Nebraska, but first we had to just find ways to keep driving. Likewise, we don't need to freak out if we hit Nebraska periods with God when nothing much changes, the radio channels all die out, boredom or relational flatness sets in, and we've run out of things to say. We can just keep driving.

But of course, sometimes Nebraska is not just boring. Sometimes Nebraska might be a nightmare that never seems to end. Sometimes God seems to have left us in Nebraska with four flats, an empty tank, and a broken GPS, and we not only don't know where He is but we can start to wonder if He ever was.

When Joseph Smith languishes for months in Liberty Jail while outlaws hound his followers, he too anguishes:

> O God, where art thou? And where is the pavilion that covereth thy hiding place?
>
> How long shall thy hand be stayed, and thine eye ... behold from the eternal heavens the wrongs of thy people and of thy servants, and thine ear be penetrated with their cries?
>
> Yea, O Lord, how long ... ? (Doctrine and Covenants 121:1–3)

In the throes of such extremities, it can be immensely challenging to just keep driving, or walking, with no assurance that we're even on the right road. When the journey hurts this much, it is understandable that we might start looking for exits to anyplace but here. As in marriage, we are most likely to call it quits with God in the Withdrawal Stage. We have hard choices to make.

When I found myself in such a stage some years ago, not knowing it was a stage but thinking it was the sudden end of the road I'd been on all my life, I was devastated to think the God I had trusted and the Church I had loved had taken me on a wild-goose chase. I had done a lot of praying, and studying, and searching, and crying while still in the power struggle, but when answers did not come, not for years, the Withdrawal Stage took over. I gradually gave up. Almost.

I still remembered those sweet, meaningful honeymoon experiences that convinced me there really was a God. I knew I could find alternative explanations for those experiences, but those alternative explanations frankly felt even more far-fetched than faith. So I kept praying, even though God never fully explained what I so desperately wanted to know. Eventually I began to wonder if I just needed to find another church. It wasn't lost on me that I had learned to pray such a prayer and expect God to answer it from the very man whose answers I now doubted. I wondered if I would have the strength to leave if God sent me elsewhere. I learned that I did have that strength, but I hated finding that out. I still wanted Joseph Smith to have been a prophet. I knew a fair amount about a lot of religions, and I knew there was good in almost all of them, but I still wanted this Church and its worldview to be true. I just didn't want it to confuse and hurt me so much.

The closest thing I got to an answer at that time was the conviction of my own experience that the Church produced good people and did good in the world, so even if it wasn't true, it probably wasn't bad. Maybe those early Church leaders weren't perfect, but I was pretty convinced that those running the Church today were at least decent people. So for a long time I stayed for our kids, hoping their faith would survive even if mine didn't. I kept going through the motions of activity. I kept accepting callings. But I kept my distance, and I kept quiet.

Ultimately I decided that divorcing God was not what I wanted, even if I had no idea how staying with Him would work. As He did with His ancient Apostles, Christ seemed to ask me, "Will ye also go away?" I wasn't nearly as sure as His Apostles were about their answer, but I felt my heart respond with them: "Lord, to whom shall [I] go? thou hast the words of eternal life" (John 6:67–68). I decided I believed in Jesus Christ. I chose to believe, even though I wasn't sure, in part because I realized people who didn't believe had just as much explaining to do as I did. I looked at my own experience, through both the good and the incredibly hard, and decided to trust that God is good, and wise, and has my best interests at heart.

And I learned that when I stayed, when I kept praying, serving, thinking, and growing, I eventually came out in . . .

The Acceptance and Renewal Stage with God

As in marriage, this stage may begin with underwhelming declarations of faith or conviction, or only tentative reinvestment in living the gospel. But we may begin to think, "There are good people here, and maybe they aren't all crazy. Maybe life wasn't great when I was praying and going to church, but it isn't great when I don't, either. Maybe I should try again. I feel really confused, even betrayed, by some things, but there are also some things here that I really value. Maybe God has His reasons for how He runs things, and maybe blackmailing Him with my anger or threats isn't helping. Maybe Church leaders are just people like me, without all the magic answers for my life, which means I'm going to have to grow up and find my own answers, which is scary. But I think God really is good, and real, and even though it doesn't all feel as cut and dried as I thought it was, it is sweet—and it is enough." We are more willing to live with the answers we do get and the inspiration that does come, even when they don't come on our timetable, in accordance with our opinions, or with the absolute certainty we thought we were entitled to.

As I settled into what I think was a deeper humility about the inherent uncertainty of mortal life, I found myself more willing to commit to my choices even though my problems didn't all get solved and I still faced plenty of distance and confusion. Eventually, when I least expected it, powerful experiences with the Spirit came, convincing evidences that went far beyond my honeymoon experiences with God. They might not have worked for anyone else, but they worked for me. I have no better intellectual answers than I ever did about some Church doctrines or policies, or why some things happened in Church history that I still don't like and still don't get, but I have felt Joseph Smith stand by my side and say, "Wendy, you know me." And I have a conviction I can't explain that that is true. In the premortal world, which he taught me exists, I trusted him once. I choose to trust him now. I believe he was, and is, a prophet of God.

Over the ensuing years, the temple has taken on deeper significance, at least much of the time. The gifts of the Spirit have become more real and varied in my life. I have learned to be more patient with human weakness, more trusting of God's power. I feel more awe at the complexity of the universe, and more peaceful about the worth to God of every single soul. I am a little less prone to argue or blame, a little more prone to repent and forgive. I am not back in Eden, but I am no longer at war, and I am no longer in despair on a lonely, endless road through Nebraska. The fruits of the Spirit are evident to me on this path. My losses are being redeemed. Although moments of uncertainty or temptation still emerge, my faith has grown deeper and my love for God inexplicably more sure. I make the choice, again and again, to believe. And I am frankly a little flabbergasted to realize, it is enough. More than enough. It is good.

The conclusions I came to in my Acceptance and Renewal Stage won't work for everyone, which is part of why I don't share them more specifically. Some of us will not move to this stage with God or the Church with our faith intact, at least not in this life. We can still be good, honest, caring, and kind. Our lives can still have meaning and purpose. Our families can still be successful. And God can still love us, help us, and talk to us. I share my personal resolution not to claim it is universal, but to make this point:

Having at least some doubts or struggles is part of the journey of a long-term, committed relationship with anyone, and those challenges don't always completely go away. But they do not have to be defining, and they do not mean that if we have any integrity at all we must call a lawyer or the bishop and get out. Sometimes there are good reasons to stay. And sometimes those good reasons turn into better reasons, even wondrous, remarkable, defining reasons, if we hold on for the ride.

If "1" is the Honeymoon Stage, "2" is the Power Struggle Stage, "3" is the Withdrawal Stage, and "4" is the Acceptance and Renewal Stage:

+ At what stage are you in your marriage or your other closest relationship right now?
+ At what stage are you in your relationship to the Church?
+ At what stage are you in your relationship with God?

If you're interested, you'll find some questions for exploring these stages in the Appendix.

In the next chapter, we'll look more closely at what the scriptures can teach us about these four stages of a relationship with God, and what we can do when we're in them to keep growing and moving forward.

Chapter 3

A MARRIED WIFE

—❦—

As the bridegroom rejoiceth over the bride,
so shall thy God rejoice over thee.

(Isaiah 62:5)

I'll admit it: sometimes I get tired of the scriptures referring so extensively to men, and I wish I didn't have to work so hard to apply them to me as a woman. Just to keep sane, I have painstakingly collected scriptures in which Jesus compares Himself to a woman, refers to Zion as "she," or calls the temple "the house of the daughters of Zion" (Doctrine and Covenants 124:11, 26–27). So I really appreciate scriptures like those above that refer to all of Israel, men and women alike, as the bride of Christ. I'm sort of sadistically grateful that when men read such verses they get to do the same mental gymnastics I have to do in order to remember how we all fit into the picture of God's relationship to man. Mankind. Humanity. Huwomanity. People. All of us. You know what I mean.

Christ claims the committed righteous as His bride, but getting married is only the beginning of a relationship we want to make eternal. We don't just want a happy wedding day. We want to be a married wife, a partner, holding on for the whole eternal union. The stages discussed in chapter 2 may help us better understand both where we've been and what is possible as we commit to give ourselves fully to God and receive Him fully in return. The lives of the great men and women in scriptures shed further light on what these stages might look like as real people attempt to claim God as their *Ishi*, their husband.

To flesh out these stages of an eternal, committed relationship with God in a little more detail, let's look at how they play out in the lives of Lehi, Laman, Lemuel, and Nephi. (And if you're a woman, remember that Lehi, Laman, Lemuel, and Nephi are all vying for the role of a bride in this story. Maybe you'll feel better.)

Lehi, Laman, Lemuel, and Nephi

Lehi, Laman, Lemuel, and Nephi are all invited by the Lord to take a journey to the promised land. But these four brides-to-be have different responses to the invitation, perhaps in part because they are in different stages of relationship with God.

Lehi is probably in something like Stage Four—Acceptance and Renewal. Presumably he has not only made his initial commitment to God but has worked through a number of challenges in bringing that relationship to maturity and fruition. His dreams and visions are not isolated events; rather, he has become a "visionary man" (1 Nephi 5:4) who has been changed by the journey and is well versed in spiritual things. He says to a worried Sariah as they wait by the Red Sea for the return of their sons from Jerusalem, "But behold, I *have obtained a land of promise*, in the which things I do rejoice" (1 Nephi 5:5). He has barely left Jerusalem, but as far as he's concerned, he has already obtained the promised land. For Lehi, the Lord's word is as good as His bond, and the promised land is not only a location but an embodiment of a relationship of complete trust in God and His promises. Lehi is like a married wife to God.

In contrast, Laman and Lemuel are unwilling to let themselves "fall in love" with God. In a way, they won't relinquish their relationship with their earthly father and brother to establish a relationship with their Heavenly Father and Brother. They continue to turn to their father's wealth, status, and stability for their sense of security rather than to their Heavenly Father, and they are deeply threatened when their father stops playing by the rules and walks away from all they stood to inherit. They are firmly in the Power Struggle Stage with their brother and earthly father for reasons we aren't fully privy to, and they never even get to the Honeymoon Stage of commitment and trust in God. They never partake of the fruit of the tree that represents God's love, and in good times or bad, whether an angel appears to them or their lives are in danger on the high seas, they don't really turn to God. They "date" God a few times, and they make the journey across the desert and the ocean to the Americas, but they never find the promised land at all. As far as they are concerned, God has never been deserving of their commitment or trust. As they face obstacles and periods of struggle, Laman and Lemuel get more argumentative, less creative, more impressed with the power of men, and less confident in the power of God. They are ever the bridesmaids, never the bride.

Nephi, on the other hand, is open to a relationship with his father's God. In fact, Nephi's relationship with his father paves the way to a covenant faith for Nephi. Trusting in his father's testimony, Nephi asks to see the vision his father saw and is shown "a tree, whose fruit was desirable to make one happy" (1 Nephi 8:10). Lehi has described this fruit as sweet above all he has ever tasted, white beyond any whiteness he has ever seen, and desirable above all other fruit (see 1 Nephi 8:11–12). Nephi adds from his own experience that it is beautiful to exceed all beauty, whiter than driven snow (see 1 Nephi 11:8), precious, and "the greatest of all the gifts of God" (1 Nephi 15:36). This tree of life is found not in the Garden of Eden but in the world, accessible to all who push past the dark mists and blinding temptations of the devil and the "vain imaginations" and mocking pride of the "large and spacious building" (1 Nephi 12:17–18), holding fast to the word of God that leads to the tree.

And what does this tree represent? "It is *the love of God*, which sheddeth itself abroad in the hearts of the children of men; where-fore, it is the most desirable above all things. . . . Yea, and the most joyous to the soul" (1 Nephi 11:22–23).

Can there be anything more important for us to seek, grasp, taste, partake of, let into our hearts and souls, and hold onto with all of our might, mind, and strength? How significant it is that Laman and Lemuel do not find the tree or partake of its fruit! They may have felt the powerful reprimand of an angel and the shock of being touched with God's power (see 1 Nephi 3:29; 17:53–54), but they do not open their hearts to feel God's love, available to all "who will have him to be their God" (1 Nephi 17:40). In contrast, Nephi tells us that despite sins and temptations, God has *"filled me with his love,* even unto the consuming of my flesh" (2 Nephi 4: 21), and Lehi shares his dying witness: ". . . a few more days and I go the way of all the earth. But behold, the Lord hath redeemed my soul from hell; I have beheld his glory, and I am encircled about eternally *in the arms of his love*" (2 Nephi 1:14–15).

Although Nephi's trust and commitment are strengthened through miraculous experiences, he also struggles with God. He debates with the Spirit about whether to kill Laban (see 1 Nephi 4:10). He is overcome by the affliction of seeing in vision the de-struction of his people (see 1 Nephi 15:5). He struggles with his brothers (see 1 Nephi 7:16), suffers with the rigors of the journey (see 1 Nephi 16:18–19), and wrestles with self-doubt and sorrow

over his temptations and sins (see 2 Nephi 4:17–18, 26–27).
Nevertheless, he eventually lands firmly in the promised land of
mature, committed trust in and love for the Lord. Even after ongoing
struggles with life, family members, and himself, Nephi writes:

> Nevertheless, I know in whom I have trusted. . . . Yea,
> I know that God will give liberally to him that asketh. Yea,
> my God will give me, if I ask not amiss; therefore I will lift
> up my voice unto thee; yea, I will cry unto thee, my God,
> the rock of my righteousness. Behold, my voice shall forever
> ascend up unto thee, my rock and mine everlasting
> God. (2 Nephi 4: 19, 35)

Nephi, Laman, and Lemuel each take a journey, but only
Nephi finds the promised land. Only Nephi is willing to fall in
love with God, commit to Him, and realize the full blessings of
becoming a married wife. He sees his relationship with his earthly
father as a stepping-stone, not an obstacle, to faith. As he takes his
journey, Nephi gets closer and closer not just to a new homeland
but to a new and everlasting covenant and home. Despite periods
of struggle with adversity and self-doubt, perhaps even periods of
distancing, boredom, or withdrawal that we are not privy to in his
record (Arabia probably feels to him a lot like Nebraska has felt to
me), Nephi stays with the journey. When Lehi's faith momentarily
falters (see 1 Nephi 16:20), Nephi looks to God, not to Lehi,
for his inheritance and security. As he faces obstacles, Nephi gets
physically stronger, more skilled and creative, and more spiritually
powerful. Nephi, like his father, Lehi, is a bride who goes the distance
of a long-term committed relationship, becoming a covenant
partner with God.

I realize that both in marriage and with God, I haven't just
gone through the stages described in chapter 2 once and then I was

done. I've seen a definite progression as I've spent years in one of the stages, then years in the next stage, but I've also cycled back and forth through these stages on varying issues for shorter or longer periods. Even when I've thought I had finally figured it out, I've found myself longing for the passion of the honeymoon, or back in a power struggle or withdrawal, needing to sort something out yet again.

I'm glad to note that Nephi doesn't just take his journey once either. Once he arrives at the promised land, he again loads up his tent to flee his brothers' wrath (see 2 Nephi 5:5–16). He unpacks his shipbuilding tools, this time to build a temple. He models his gold plates after the brass plates he obtained at such cost in Jerusalem. He uses his sword to defend his people from new enemies. He wrestles again with the Lord over the welfare of his soul. But the journey is a little less arduous and lengthy the second time around.

Life before Commitment

As Laman and Lemuel demonstrate, not everyone chooses to fall in love with God at all. There is actually a "Precommitment Stage" in a relationship, including in a relationship with God—a stage before we decide to make a commitment we intend to keep. A question to consider in the Precommitment Stage with God is, "Are you willing to let God's love in? Are you willing to commit to loving and trusting Him?"

One of the most important decisions we make is whether we believe purpose and goodwill underpin the existence of the universe. There is plenty of evidence on both sides of that question. If we decide to trust there is a "friendly" God who is good, wise, and in charge, then we get to decide whether to sign up for the incredible journey to our personal promised land of a thriving and joyous relationship with Him. Chances are that journey will include moments of indescribable beauty as well as moments of struggling, feeling overwhelmed, and wondering if we are up to the trip. But countless prophets and ordinary people testify that the destination is worth the effort and that the trip itself is amazing.

If we have been disappointed in human relationships, however—and who hasn't?—it can be hard not to bring our expectations of disappointment to our relationship with God. We may be afraid to get our hopes up. We may think we need a dramatic, powerful, undeniable demonstration of His trustworthiness and accessibility before we are willing to commit. We may worry that we will be deceived, that we aren't good enough, or that it will be too hard. God understands our fears, and He works with us wherever we are. But He also needs us to at least consider the possibility that His love is real.

We may wonder, however, "Does God really want closeness with me? Because it surely seems like a lot of the time He keeps His distance." Even when we believe His invitation is sincere, there are times we might wonder, "Can I afford to trust that my longing for Him is reciprocated, that He won't lure me into a commitment and a love He doesn't fully return? What is the evidence that He really wants to love and care for me? It often seems He doesn't pay much attention to me at all." Or perhaps, "I think God wants more closeness with me than I'm really up for. It feels like He just has a lot of expectations. If I sign up for this relationship, is God going to get all mushy and demanding on me? Or is He really going to help me?" We instinctively know that the person who commits the most has the most to lose. We don't want to lose.

When we rely on our own imaginations about who God is, we have only our old templates of past injuries with relationships to inform us. If we begin instead with scriptures and direct experience with God, we have a better chance of perceiving God's workings in our life more accurately. As we learn from the scriptures who God is, we are better able to look for and receive the evidences of His love for us today.

Consider the following scriptural evidences of how the Father and the Savior feel about us and the relationship They desire with us:

> Incline your ear, and come unto me: hear, and your soul shall live; and I will make an everlasting covenant with you. (Isaiah 55:3)
>
> O Jerusalem, Jerusalem ... how often [have I desired to gather] thy children together, even as a hen gathereth her chickens under her wings. (Matthew 23:37; see footnote c)
>
> Jesus answered ... If a man love me, he will keep my words: and my Father will love him, and we will come unto him, and make our abode with him. (John 14:23)
>
> Behold, I stand at the door, and knock: if any man hear my voice, and open the door, I will come in to him, and will sup with him, and he with me. (Revelation 3:20)
>
> And ... the Lord of the vineyard wept, and said ... What could I have done more for my vineyard? ... I have nourished it, and I have digged about it, and I have pruned it, and I have dunged it; and I have stretched forth mine hand almost all the day long . (Jacob 5:41, 47)
>
> Draw near unto me and I will draw near unto you; seek me diligently and ye shall find me. (Doctrine and Covenants 88:63)

"Come unto Me"

For me, one of the most striking aspects of the Book of Mormon account of Christ's visit to the American continent is how often the Savior repeats the injunction, "Come unto me." This phrase is repeated fifteen times in the few chapters of 3 Nephi that recount His visit, while the same phrase never appears more than twice in any of the four gospels of the New Testament. While there may be many reasons for this difference, perhaps one reason is that Jesus's suffering during His Atonement and Crucifixion have made Him in a deeper, more personal way "[a] high priest which [can] be touched with the feeling of our infirmities" (Hebrews 4:15). Speaking to the survivors of three hours of horrific, widespread destruction and three days without any shred of light that have left them "howling," "weeping," and "groaning" continually for their brothers, mothers, daughters, and children who have died, and after He has listed city after city that has been burned, sunk, or buried, the next words of the Savior—fresh from His own hours of indescribable suffering and empathy-magnifying darkness—are His pleading appeal to the survivors to come close:

> O all ye that are spared because ye were more righteous than they, will ye not now *return unto me*, and repent of your sins, and be converted, that *I may heal you?*
>
> Yea, verily I say unto you, if ye will *come unto me* ye shall have eternal life. Behold, *mine arm of mercy is extended towards you*, and whosoever will come, *him will I receive;* and blessed are those who *come unto me.* (3 Nephi 9:13–14)

When He comes in person among these wounded and grief-weary survivors, who are still amazed by the extent of their losses but apparently have responded from their hearts to His call to repent, He doesn't just stand up in the sky and shout instructions. He doesn't show up as some fuzzy apparition or come into their minds as an abstract quality. He comes as a real person and says to them in both words and deeds, "Come to me! See my face. Hear the timbre of my voice as I pray for you and with you. Let me teach you and call you by name. Touch my scars with your fingers. Let me touch you and heal you. Let me hear your most intimate thoughts. Let me feel with you your deepest grief and heartache. Let me make your children my children. Let me minister to you, feed you, and surround you with the evidences of my love." He doesn't just want them to obey Him out of fear or duty; He wants them to know Him, have a relationship with Him, trust Him, love Him, and join Him in His work of salvation among them. He introduces the Father to them, alluding to His Father an average of once for every two verses recording His words. He invites them to pray to the Father and establish a relationship of love and trust with Him, reminding them repeatedly that He, His Father, and the Holy Ghost are one (see 3 Nephi 11:27, 32, 36).

Once, as I was contemplating this story, I was particularly struck with the intimacy with which Christ prays. These prayers are so tender, compassionate, and powerful that "no tongue can speak, neither can there be written by any man, neither can the hearts of men conceive so great and marvelous things as we both saw and heard Jesus speak; and no one can conceive of the joy which filled our souls at the time we heard him pray for us unto the Father" (3 Nephi 17:17). He didn't pray for them in some global way. I'm guessing that what filled their hearts with such joy and awe was that He prayed for them by name, by circumstance, with a personal awareness of them that defied their understanding and taught them at a level even beneath words that He knew them personally and loved them deeply. I felt what has been called holy envy as I wondered what it would have felt like to have the Savior pray for me.

A few verses later I read: "And now Father, I pray unto thee for them, and also for all those who shall believe on their words, that they may believe in me, that I may be in them as thou, Father, art in me, that we may be one" (3 Nephi 19:23; see also John 17:20).

As I read these words, I was somewhat dumbstruck to realize that, over 2,000 years later, I was included in Christ's prayer. I am one who "believe[s] on their words." Could it be that Christ, now as then, knows me by name and prays to the Father for me? As I pondered that thought, I heard the words clearly in my mind, "I pray for you all the time." I am still awed by such a possibility. But it also seems obvious that Jesus would pray for me. He has suffered for me; He is my Advocate with the Father; He is my Brother and Friend.

If Christ prays for me, He prays for you. Christ prays to the Father for your children, your friends. He knows their names. He prays for your healing, your growth; He joins in your sorrows, your joys. I believe that. If you don't, you might consider asking God if it is true.

We are in a phase of our eternal existence in which we are separated from Those who love us most, that we might grow and learn by our own experience. But Their words to the prophet Enoch about the end of this mortal existence epitomize for me Their tender and affectionate longing to be close to us:

> Righteousness and truth will I cause to sweep the earth as with a flood, to gather out mine elect from the four quarters of the earth. . . . And the Lord said unto Enoch: Then shalt thou and all thy city meet them there, and we [the Father, the Son, Enoch, and his people] *will receive them into our bosom, and they shall see us; and we will fall upon their necks, . . . and we will kiss each other; And there shall be mine abode.* (Moses 7:62–64)

This is the longing, joyful love of a father, a brother, a husband and friend, waiting with great anticipation to embrace and kiss and welcome us home.

If you haven't yet opened up your heart to fall in love with God, consider getting on your knees tonight and simply telling Him what you're afraid of, if you know, or asking Him to help you figure it out if you don't.

Tips for Stage One: The Honeymoon

If you have at least made it to the Honeymoon Stage with God, congratulations. I hope you've written down experiences you have had with His Spirit that helped you make that commitment so you will remember and savor them throughout your life. Just as the Nephites would have perished in unbelief without access to the scriptures (see 1 Nephi 4:12–17), we perish spiritually when we do not remember, reflect on, and learn from our personal experiences with Deity. Consider taking a few minutes each night, each Sunday, each month, or each year, to record these experiences as your personal "scriptures."

I am grateful to Kathleen Flake for pointing out to me that at His last Passover meal with His Apostles, hours before His Crucifixion, Christ gives them a concrete way to remember their last sacred experiences with Him. As He institutes the sacrament at the Last Supper, it is as if He is saying, "Things are going to get bad now. You're going to wonder what in the world is going on. You're going to doubt and fear. I want you to remember then what you're feeling now. I want you to hold on to this sweet moment when those hard moments come." Specifically, in the Joseph Smith Translation of Mark 14:21–24, Christ tells the Apostles at the Last Supper that whenever they partake of the bread and wine they should "remember this hour that I was with you. . . . And as oft as ye do this ordinance, ye will remember me in this hour that I was with you." Likewise, in 3 Nephi 18:7, He tells the Nephites to partake of the sacrament "in remembrance of my body, which I have shown unto you."

What have been your sacred suppers with the Lord? What did you experience? What has He told you? How have you felt? These are your living evidences of His commitment to you, and you will need to remember them through all the stages that lie ahead. You don't have to just dwell on His suffering, or on yours. You can also remember the sweet hours that He has been with you, feeding you, preparing you, teaching you. The testimonies and faith-promoting experiences of others can also help you remember, feel, and culti-vate the sweetness of the Honeymoon Stage with God.

* Ponder: Am I willing to fall in love with God?
* Write down your love story with God.
* Use the sacrament to remember the hours He has been with you.

Tips for Stage Two: The Power Struggle

God can take our honest concerns and frustrations. But pre-senting our frustrations to God with whining, shame, blame, self-pity, and resentment—blackmailing God with our misery or an-ger—these simply don't work. Trust me, I've tried them all. Growth requires us to wean ourselves off of these defensive choices and to humbly say with the man who sought a miracle from the Savior, "Lord, I believe; help thou mine unbelief" (Mark 9:24).

One of the hardest internal wrestles I sometimes face is with the notion that God can save even me, with all my faults and fears. There is a voice in my head that I can mistake for the Lord's voice. It tells me how guilty I should feel, how broken I am, how much others wouldn't like me if they really knew me. Tellingly, Satan is referred to in Revelation 12:10 as "the accuser of our brethren . . . which accused them before our God day and night." Satan doesn't accuse the unrighteous, but "brethren"—those who choose to be-lieve. I've begun to notice that the tone and quality of the voice in my head are good indicators of who is really speaking to me. If the voice in my mind is sarcastic, angry, mocking, or accusing, if it seems disgusted with me, if it calls me names or belittles, if it makes me feel ashamed or hopeless, it is not the voice of God. I can, and should, ignore it. Satan is my accuser, and he accuses me even to me.

In contrast, Christ is called our advocate (see 1 John 2:1; Doctrine and Covenants 29:5). An advocate is a person who is on our side, who argues our case, who presents us in the best possible light. Christ will not lie for us, but as long as we are not lying to ourselves He will correct us with persuasion, long-suffering, gentleness, meekness, and love unfeigned (see Doctrine and Covenants 121:41). His is a voice we can trust because it offers us direction, even correction, without accusation or shaming that lead to despair. With Christ as our advocate, we can afford to develop a playful heart, try new approaches, keep a sense of humor, and not give up.

I've also learned that, as in marriage, I may influence God but I can't change Him. The one person I can change is me, and that is difficult enough. I have my own 69 percent of weaknesses and problems that I will probably struggle with all my life before I even get to my relationship challenges. But as I choose to believe in God, the power struggle shifts from a struggle against God to a struggle *with me and God united* against my doubts, sins, worries, and unrealistic expectations.

Perhaps it is not by accident that we are called the children of Israel—Israel being the name God gave to Jacob after his personal struggle or wrestle with God. Jacob has been told by the Lord to take his wives and children and return to the land of his fathers, but when he sends word of his impending arrival to his brother Esau, who has been his adversary, the messengers return with word that Esau is en route with four hundred men. This isn't a welcoming party but an army, and Jacob is "greatly afraid and distressed" (Genesis 32:7). He pleads with God, in words we might relate to in the power struggle:

> O God of my father Abraham . . . the Lord which saidst unto me, Return unto thy country, and to thy kindred, and I will deal well with thee:
>
> I am not worthy of the least of all the mercies, and of all the truth, which thou has shewed unto thy servant; for with my staff I passed over this Jordan; and now I am become two bands.
>
> Deliver me, I pray thee, from the hand of my brother, from the hand of Esau: for I fear him, lest he will come and smite me, and the mother with the children.
>
> And thou saidst, I will surely do thee good, and make thy seed as the sand of the sea, which cannot be numbered for multitude. (Genesis 32:9–12)

I would probably put it more bluntly: "You are the one who told me to go home, and now look what's happened! You've got to do something!" Knowing that in some ways Esau's anger toward him is justified, but also knowing that God has promised blessings, Jacob wrestles all night with an unidentified messenger whom Jacob tells, "I will not let thee go, except thou bless me" (Genesis 32:26). The "man" tells Jacob: "Thy name shall be called no more Jacob [meaning *the supplanter*, or even *the deceiver*], but Israel [*one who struggles with God and prevails*]: for as a prince hast thou power with God and with men, and hast prevailed" (Genesis 32:28).

Although the messenger will not tell Jacob his name, Jacob "called the name of the place Peniel [*the face of God*]: for I have seen God face to face, and my life is preserved" (Genesis 32:30).

We, as the children of Israel, may rightly claim Israel's name when we are willing to wrestle with the Lord as Israel (Jacob) did. Like him, we wrestle not for an hour but until the light breaks and we prevail by allowing God to prevail with us. We do all we can to trust that we will obtain, that God will bless us, and that He will fulfill the promises He has given us in His own time and in His own way and according to His own will.

Maybe we won't fully understand polygamy for a few decades, or same-sex attraction, or why we felt so good about marrying someone who deeply betrayed us. We may have to work around such things, keep our sense of humor, get help from other people, and expect to gradually understand them better over time. Like Jacob confronted with Esau's army when he had been promised God's blessing, we may be confused and frustrated—we may want God to know He can't just ignore the promises we think He's made and not fulfilled. This can be a crazy-making period of our growing up in God. As one person told me in the throes of the Power Struggle, "I literally feel like I'll lose my mind if I can't get some answers." Even if we don't fully understand in our lifetime, our willingness to engage the wrestle is sometimes a necessary precursor to attaining the blessing.

+ Replace whining, shame, and blackmail with self-compassion, humility, and honesty
+ Notice the quality of the voice in your head so you can ignore the accuser and trust the advocate
+ Be willing to wrestle until the light breaks, even if you have to take a few naps

Tips for Stage Three: Withdrawal

People don't seem to talk much about the Withdrawal Stage in the scriptures. Maybe it doesn't quite register as something worth writing down compared to the mighty wrestles of Enoch, Enos,

Hagar, or Esther, or the powerful spiritual experiences of Mary, Abraham, Abish, or the brother of Jared. But lessons can come in the Withdrawal Stage that we may not be open to at other times.

In a recent flat period in my relationship with God, I pled with God to help me improve my relationship with Him. I prayed about this for many months but received little or no response from God. Nebraska! Finally I did get one pretty clear message: "Work on your relationship with your husband. Then we'll talk." Hmmm.

Well, I didn't want to work on my relationship with my husband. In fact, my relationship with my husband was just fine. A little distant, but fine. But I needed to learn to *tolerate a deeper level of intimacy* by practicing it with a fellow mortal before I was prepared for the closeness I longed for with God.

The practice I think I've needed is not just about learning skills for communicating better or going on more dates. The practice I needed, and need, is about learning to tolerate the vulnerability I feel when I risk failing at something I care about, or when I allow someone to see me as I am with all my flaws and strengths. It includes learning to tolerate praying differently from the person I'm praying with, or admitting I'm still afraid of stupid stuff that happened decades ago, or acknowledging I was wrong.

For someone else an equivalent message might be to work on your relationship with your bishop, parent, sibling, child, missionary companion, or people you date. But we don't learn to tolerate intimacy all by ourselves. It takes two to learn to tango.

A friend of mine also noted about her own long drives through Nebraska (literally) that in the absence of all the stimulation of billboards, traffic, or breathtaking scenery, little things she would normally have ignored began to stand out more. She noticed and delighted in subtle differences in the color of the sky. A lizard crossing the road became a source of delight and long conversation.

A root beer was savored as never before. In a similar way, our spiritual Nebraskas can teach us to tune into even the smallest spiritual promptings, be more grateful for any hint of a blessing, and become more sensitive to the finer details of our obedience.

In the Withdrawal Stage, our best course is generally simply to stay the course. We keep praying, asking God to help us see ourselves more clearly, to help us not whine, and to help us not fall asleep at the wheel as we plod through Nebraska. We keep reading the scriptures—those given to the Church, and those we have recorded as our personal scriptures. We remember the times God was with us—our Last Supper experiences—so that when the clouds roll in, the soldiers advance, and the God we trusted seems to have forsaken us we don't give up. We keep living our values—what we personally claim and believe to be good. We may not understand all truth, but we can generally figure out what is good, and Moroni teaches us that "whatsoever thing is *good* is . . . *true*" (Moroni 10:6).

- Work on intimacy with other human beings.
- Practice tolerating vulnerability and fear, rather than trying to avoid them at all costs.
- Pay more attention to and express more gratitude for the little signs of God's presence.
- Just keep driving, even when the road feels long and desolate.

Stage Four: Life in the Acceptance and Renewal Stage

I'm not completely sure if there is some final, ultimate Acceptance and Renewal Stage that I will attain with God in this life. Sometimes I think I get there, but then I pop back into a power struggle or withdrawal again without always knowing why. But I believe, and increasingly experience, that this stage is both possible and deeply desirable. My guess from such experience as I've had is that the Acceptance and Renewal Stage entails transcending, not solving, our problems, somehow stepping out of the pendulum swing between power struggle and withdrawal, or dichotomies like powerful/weak, close/distant, love/leave, male/female, or good/bad.

Here are some of the things this stage means to me so far:

- Gradually choosing to see the ways God's ways are truly higher than my ways (see Isaiah 55:9), even while I cherish learning by my own experience.
- Becoming more realistic in my expectations of other people, of Church leaders, of myself, and of God without giving up my power or my hope.
- Deciding God doesn't owe me after all, and starting to see how much I owe Him.
- Trusting more deeply than ever that He will make good on His promises once I understand them more deeply.
- Trying less to get Him to do what I want, and wanting to more truly learn what He wants—while willingly doing the hard spiritual and psychological work of figuring out my answers to the question, "What desirest thou?" (1 Nephi 11:2; see also Ether 2:25).
- Becoming more aware of my own untrustworthiness, hopefully making me both more trustworthy and more able to appreciate the trustworthiness of God.
- Engaging more creatively and passionately in God's work and engaging Him more in mine.
- Becoming more humble, more willing to ask, more open to help, and more willing to help others.
- Submitting my will to His more wholeheartedly, joyfully, and gratefully.

When my relationship with God reminds me of an old married couple eating in silence with nothing they care to share, I can remember and renew my honeymoon passion for God, now with a deeper and more meaningful sense of awe. When I am frustrated or confused, I can engage my power struggles with Him with more self-awareness and integrity about the flaws in my heart, and with less shame, or anger, or fear of God abandoning me to my sins. When vast lulls stop my forward motion, I can endure silence with a calmer and more trusting faith and accept a more still, small voice in answer to my prayers, even when the answer is simply "no." The absolute certainty I thought others had "without a shadow of a doubt" still eludes me at times, and yet my love for Him has more reality, depth, and wonder than I have words to express. I can testify with Nephi, "I know in whom I have trusted. My God hath been my support; he hath led me through mine afflictions. . . . He hath filled me with his love, even unto the consuming of my flesh. . . . He hath heard my cry by day, and he hath given me knowledge by visions in the night-time. . . . O Lord, I have trusted in thee, and I will trust in thee forever" (2 Nephi 4:19–21, 23, 34).

The Pot and the Potter

Even though God loves us as personally and deeply as a father loves a child, the distance between His wisdom and ours really is like the distance between the wisdom of a lump of clay and the wisdom of a master potter (see Isaiah 64:8; Jeremiah 18:6). Disconnected from the Vine, we will not be free (as we sometimes imagine); rather we will wither and die (see John 15:6). Our relationship with God is not yet a marriage of equals; we owe Christ all that we have and are (see John 15:5).

And yet, remarkably, God doesn't just shape us like clay or herd us like sheep or order us about like slaves. He asks us what we want. He honors our desires and agency (see 1 Nephi 11:2; Ether 2:25). He invites us into the creative process with Him, offering to seal us to the spouse *we* choose and to help us with the work *we* love (see Doctrine and Covenants 132:19). He doesn't just tell us His predetermined plan for our life, but He invites us, even in our oh-so-limited and infantile state, to work with Him to claim our dreams and fulfill them (see Doctrine and Covenants 58:27; 137:9). He doesn't just ask us to build His kingdom, but also He teaches us true principles and lets us build our own (see Moses 1:6, 25). Even though we are but foolish children who cannot see afar off, He sends us out to create, to lead out, and to build relationships worth perpetuating for eternity—and *He* joins *us* in our efforts every bit as much as the other way around (see Doctrine and Covenants 132:46).

He doesn't just turn us into pots, but He makes us potters (see Doctrine and Covenants 132:20).

This makes no sense. It is unfathomable. But it is how the omnipotent, holy God stands humbly before our agency, offering us His heart and His help in navigating the complexities of using that agency well (see Moses 7:32–33).

How do we not fall in love with such a God?

(Note: See the Appendix for some questions and exercises relevant to each of these stages as they may apply to our relationship with God.)

Section Two

CONNECTING WITH GOD

Chapter 4

DISCOVERING OUR RELATIONSHIP ASSUMPTIONS

*And that wicked one cometh and taketh away light
and truth, through disobedience, from the children of
men, and because of the tradition of their fathers.*

(Doctrine and Covenants 93:39)

In section one of this book, exploring the four common stages of long-term committed relationships hopefully helped us better understand some of the inevitable ups and downs in our relationship with God. We noticed that power struggles and times of distance can be potentially valuable indicators of what we yet need to learn. If we are willing to grow and change, not merely go along for a ride, we can be more than a pot, a sheep, or a servant—we can become an eternal partner with the God who invites us close.

As we proceed through the relationship journey, however, we won't deepen our trust in God unless we increasingly see Him as He really is, not as we imagine Him to be. What we've learned from our past can blur our vision without our even knowing it. Like fish unable to see the water they swim in, we may struggle to see the personal worldview we operate in. That worldview, shaped by our history and experience, can deeply affect how we perceive God and what we expect from Him.

When Christ teaches the Lord's Prayer to those He invites to come unto Him, He reminds us that prayer is the quintessential form for expressing, receiving, and developing a relationship with God. The Lord's Prayer is more than a ritual or a form to fill in as we pray. Elements of the Lord's Prayer can also help us understand how our relationship with God is negatively or positively affected by expectations we've learned from our past experience.

Following an outline implied in the Lord's Prayer, the remaining chapters of this book will explore:

+ Hidden assumptions about relationships that affect how we see God (this chapter)
+ Drawing on God's compassion to turn our story into a more objective history (chapter 5)
+ How our fears about the future can impact our trust in the Lord (chapter 6)
+ How we can more gratefully receive and live in the present moment with God (chapter 7)
+ Ways to detect and reject temptation and sin in order to draw closer to Deity (chapter 8)
+ Emulating the holy roles of Creator, Redeemer, and Messenger in God's kingdom (chapter 9)

The Impact of Early Relationships

As the scripture quoted at the start of this chapter reminds us, the traditions of the fathers have an impact in people's lives. When Jesus taught His disciples the now-familiar phrase, "Our Father which art in heaven, Hallowed be thy name" (3 Nephi 13:9; Matthew 6:9), He reminded them and us of our true identity as children of a loving and holy Father. But we do more than *invoke* our Father's name when we pray. We also *evoke* a host of memories about fathers and mothers and relationships in general, traditions of our fathers and mothers that leave us with a host of

After this manner therefore pray ye:

Our Father which art in heaven,
Hallowed be thy name.
Thy kingdom come.
Thy will be done in earth,
as it is in heaven.

Give us this day our daily bread.
And forgive us our debts,
as we forgive our debtors.

And lead us not into temptation,
but deliver us from evil:
For thine is the kingdom,
and the power,
and the glory, for ever.
Amen.

MATTHEW 6:9–13

expectations about how relationships work. We evoke assumptions about how safe or vulnerable we are in relationships, whether they are threatening or helpful, of value or irrelevant. We learn these expectations primarily in the context of early family and social experiences in which we decide how much to trust, what disappointments are likely, and how to get our needs met. These assumptions can profoundly but unconsciously influence how we experience God and what we think we mean to Him. And they are often consciously and unconsciously passed from one generation to the next. Raymond (I call him that because, truly, everybody loves him) shares his experience:

> It is hard to admit at church amid this parade of people talking about God's love that I feel distant from God. But if I were to sum up where my biggest challenges have been over the years it would be my frustration over not feeling God's love for me. I can bear testimony of the Book of Mormon, of Joseph Smith, even of feeling the Spirit, but I don't see God walking hand in hand through life with me. I don't know this deeply loving God.
>
> A few years ago in a Sunday School class the teacher mentioned a study in which people were asked to sum up God in one word. He asked the class what we would say. In the study and in the class, a high percentage of people said "love." But the first word that came to my mind was "judge." That got my attention, so I asked my siblings and my parents what they would say. Basically, they all said "judge." We all see God as this grumpy old judge.
>
> When I was a kid, Mom was this super righteous returned missionary who wanted everything perfect. Dad was a Church leader, but was later excommunicated, became agnostic, and my parents divorced. I grew up thinking the

minute you sin, it's over for you. You've forever lost the ideal you. If you're not a General Authority who has had your calling and election made sure by the time you're thirty God really isn't interested in you. If children project onto God what their parents are like, I've done that in spades. But I don't know how to change that. It goes beyond reason and understanding. It seems to be how I'm wired.

I especially worry about my siblings. My brother struggled with this issue for years and he finally threw up his hands and gave up. It ruined his family, but he says the only way he's found any peace is by being an atheist. I don't know why I'm still hanging in there. I guess I saw what my parents' and brother's choices did to their families and I didn't want to create that kind of pain for my kids. I just choose to believe, I choose faith, which I somehow can do despite this God problem. I do family history, and I go to the temple, and I pray like crazy that my ancestors will accept this and go to my siblings and help them. They're in agony all the time, and I can't help them. Maybe our ancestors can.

I have to say I don't understand the Atonement. I don't think it is that I don't understand the doctrine. I just do not see it as a force in my life. I know the Atonement is supposed to reconnect us to God, but why should we need an advocate with our own Father? It doesn't sound like the Father is on my side if He needs Jesus to convince Him to let me back in the house.

Maybe for some people it just is not possible to really feel the love we want because this feeling of judgment is so ingrained. I find it really hard to really go forward with confidence in life because I honestly believe God wants me to fail. I'm not perfect so God's disappointed. I wish I knew what it would feel like to feel really accepted for who I am, for trying.

I'm in a lot of conflict.[1]

Raymond's story reminds us that although our experience with our fellow mortals is inevitably inadequate as a template for relating to our perfect Heavenly Father, we have to start somewhere as we try to imagine what to expect from God and what He might expect from us. As a result, we may assume God expects perfection because our parents did, even when our rational brain thinks otherwise. We may unconsciously look for and even create evidences that God is not trustworthy because our fellow humans have taught us that trust is dangerous. We may fear God because we've been hurt, long for God because we've been lonely, or distance ourselves from God because we believe we can only safely rely on ourselves. When God invites us close, we may prefer to stay away if closeness feels like a precursor to painful loss. We may cling and plead if clinging and pleading are the only things that have succeeded in the past. Or we may try to manipulate God with the professed incompetence or the open rage we've used elsewhere to try to get other people to meet our needs.

How Do You Experience God?

Understanding our relationship predispositions can help us stop blaming God (or anyone else, for that matter) for conflicts or distances we may unwittingly expect and even contribute to. The following questionnaire offers an informal way to ponder some of your expectations and assumptions about God. No one is looking over your shoulder, so take the risk to note how you really think and feel. You may learn more if you rate these items based on how you feel during hard times, not just when things are sailing along nicely.

Look over the following sentences. Rate EACH ITEM in EACH GROUP as follows:

- ◆ 0 for "I rarely if ever feel this way"
- ◆ 1 for "I sometimes feel this way"
- ◆ 2 for "I fairly often feel this way"
- ◆ 3 for "I generally feel this way"

A. Communicating with God

_____ 1. I plead for direction and help, but I worry that I don't receive as many answers as I want.

_____ 2. I assume God doesn't care much about the little details of my life.

_____ 3. I don't know how to figure out what God wants or thinks, and I've given up trying.

_____ 4. I regularly receive quiet spiritual direction or help.

B. Meeting God's expectations

_____ 1. I want to please God, but I'm afraid I cannot keep up with all He expects.

_____ 2. I figure out my own life because I don't think God cares that much what we do.

_____ 3. I find God's expectations unfair, abusive, and hurtful.

_____ 4. I want to learn what God expects from me and feel confident that He will help me do it.

C. God's assessment of me

_____ 1. I try to serve and obey, but I'm guessing God is pretty disappointed with me.

_____ 2. I assume God is more or less okay with what I choose, but I don't really ask.

_____ 3. God isn't really there for me, so why should I care what He thinks of me.

_____ 4. I believe God trusts me to make good choices and that He is pleased with my life.

D. God's availability

_____ 1. God is not as responsive or as involved with my life as I wish He were.

_____ 2. I don't really expect God to get involved in the day-to-day details of my life.

_____ 3. When I've needed Him most, God hasn't protected me or helped me.

_____ 4. I experience God as accessible, interested, and willing to respond to my prayers.

E. Feeling God's love

_____ 1. It would mean everything to me to feel God's love for me personally, but I don't really.

_____ 2. I've been taught that God loves us all, and that's enough for me.

_____ 3. I'm not excited about getting close to a God who let me be deceived, betrayed, or abused.

_____ 4. I find comfort in remembering meaningful experiences I've had of feeling God's love for me.

F. God and stress

_____ 1. When I am overstressed, God can feel like a critical taskmaster I can never please.

_____ 2. When life gets really busy, I tend to forget about connecting with God.

_____ 3. When life feels overwhelming, I certainly can't count on God to understand or help.

_____ 4. When I have too much to do, God feels like a helpful resource.

G. Handling God's silences

_____ 1. When I can't get answers from God, I feel abandoned, distressed, and alone.

_____ 2. I'm pretty independent and self-sufficient, so I don't mind that much when God is quiet.

_____ 3. If there is a God, He is not someone I can depend on or turn to.

_____ 4. When God feels far away, I trust that He is still aware of me and will return in His time.

H. God and suffering

_____ 1. When I feel loss or pain I anxiously plead with God for help, but comfort and reassurance are slow to come.

_____ 2. When I feel loss or pain, I assume God expects me to "buck up" and move on.

_____ 3. When I feel loss or pain, trying to connect with God and failing only makes it worse.

_____ 4. When I feel loss or pain, God comforts me both directly and through other people.

When you are finished, add up your scores for all of the #1 items, then for all the #2 items, etc.

Total for #1 items: _____

Total for #2 items: _____

Total for #3 items: _____

Total for #4 items: _____

If your highest score is for the #1 items, you may have an **Anxious Attachment Style** with God.

If your highest score is for the #2 items, you may have an **Avoidant Attachment Style** with God.

If your highest score is for the #3 items, you may have a **Traumatic Attachment Style** with God.

If your highest score is for the #4 items, you may have a **Secure Attachment Style** with God.

Whichever category of attachment style you fall into, you'll find a brief explanation of that style below. I'll also explain more about how our attachment style develops and how it predisposes us to expect certain things in our relationship with God. I realize this can sound like so much psychobabble, but the reason for taking the time to explore attachment styles is that some of what we learn from our attachment style can help us see God more accurately and trust Him more deeply, while some of it can get in our way.

But first, what exactly is an attachment style? Here's a little background.

A Theory of Attachment

One of the great privileges of my life was the opportunity to hear the late John Bowlby present his ideas about "attachment" to students and faculty at the University of Michigan.[2] Although he helped the world understand the importance of warm, loving bonds, Bowlby was a somewhat aloof, proper, stoic, British psychiatrist whose own attachment history was pretty shaky. However, his work with orphans after World War II changed the way people think about child development, child rearing, marital relationships, and psychotherapy. His work still reverberates through all of those fields. As new techniques for imaging brain activity have developed, we can see pictures of confirming evidence for many of Bowlby's once-controversial theories. It turns out that warm, secure bonds in our early years literally change the structure, flexibility, and functioning of our developing brains.

Whether or not you recognize John Bowlby's name, his ideas

affect how you live. Thanks to Bowlby's work, along with decades of research by many people, parents no longer drop young children off at sanitariums and come back a month later when they are cured to pick them up, expecting them to have a stiff upper lip about the long separation. Ronald McDonald Houses have sprung up near hospitals, foster care has taken the place of orphanages, boarding schools for elementary school children have declined, and hospice care has replaced hospitals for the dying—all because of his influence. Bowlby helped us understand that children need consistently warm and available parents, adults need available and responsive spouses and friends, and the elderly need affection and family bonds to manage the vicissitudes of life. We don't all get what we need, to be sure, but getting this kind of stable care is what helps us gain courage and confidence in a shaky world. Although we may take some of these trends too far (stifling the growing independence of older children, for example), Bowlby helped us see that we are most likely to grow, learn, and function well when securely attached to people who hold us, delight in us, and engage us warmly and consistently.

Bowlby believed that human beings come hardwired to attach to other human beings. Psychologist Mary Ainsworth tested and developed his theories, beginning with toddlers.[3] A child's connection to parents provides a secure base from which the child can explore the world and a safe haven to which the child can return to regroup when the world is too frightening or hard. Children whose parents are consistently available, responsive, and engaged grow up with different relationship templates and expectations—and quite literally with different brains—from children who, for whatever reason, are not so secure.

Children bring their own personalities and temperaments to these family ties, making it easier for parents to connect with some children than others. Children with autism may actively avoid attachment to people despite engaged and caring parents, and some especially anxious children are difficult to console or reassure enough. Children also have experiences independent of their parents that affect their attachment style, and that help or hinder their relationship skills. But our early relationship templates can affect our assumptions about relationships for years to come. It follows that they may also affect our relationship with God.[4]

Attachment Styles

Borrowing from Bowlby and others who have expanded on his work, let's consider four basic attachment styles.[5] To make this easier to understand, I'll start with the last style listed in the exercise above, the secure attachment style, then go in order for the rest, as follows:

4. Secure
1. Anxious
2. Avoidant
3. Traumatic

The explanations below alternate between "he" and "she," but obviously both men and women fall into all of these styles.

Style #4: Secure. In terms of children's well-being, the most desirable attachment style is secure attachment. Most of us have at least some of these characteristics at least some of the time, especially when we are feeling safe. Which aspects of a secure attachment are typical of you, and which would you like to develop more? Take a look:

How it starts. A "secure attachment" begins developing in infancy as parents regularly look into a baby's eyes, cuddle him, soothe him, talk to him, smile at him, and respond to his unspoken needs. A securely attached toddler likes being close to his parents and sees them as a safe haven. When left temporarily, he may protest and search around, but a friendly outsider can get him interested in a new toy until Mom comes back. When she does, he'll want reassurance and reconnection, but after a few minutes he can leave Mom's side and go looking for the toys again. Mom and Dad provide a secure home base from which to explore the world.

How it develops. As he grows up, a securely attached kid learns to feel worthy of help and love whether he is happy or distressed. He has a sense of competence and worth and trusts people to like him and help him. He likes playing, exploring, and creating. He isn't especially prone to mental illnesses, and he has an easier time riding through the inevitable bumps and dips of life. He can say what he needs, work out problems with other people, and apologize and forgive. He doesn't tend to either idealize or demonize himself or other people. He may be either an introvert (who thrives on solitude) or an extrovert (who gets a kick out of social interaction), but he generally enjoys and gets along with others.

How might a secure attachment style impact our relationship with God? Compared to people with other styles, we would generally expect the securely attached adult to have an easier time trusting God's love even when God seems unavailable right now. Secure in his human relationships, he will probably more easily trust that God has his best interests at heart. He probably finds solace and strength in faith. He may have times when he's angry, withdrawn, or anxious with God, but we would expect him to bounce back more readily. Even though he'll have his share of challenges, being securely attached should help him overcome them.

+ Which of these characteristics do you have and which would you especially like to develop further?

Style #1: Anxious. The first of the less desirable attachment styles is anxious attachment. Some elements of this style may show up in most of us if we are under enough stress, so even if this isn't your predominant style, take a look.

How it starts. A child with an anxious attachment style generally has parents who are not as consistently warm or available, often because they have too much stress in their own lives—things like illness, anxiety, or having to move a lot. Poverty is especially hard on parents and children, and it is a big factor in all kinds of attachment problems. This child may also have been born with a body that is more easily startled or with a physical illness that makes it harder for parents to "read" or soothe her, leaving her feeling unsettled even when her parents are trying hard to help. That can make her parents more anxious as well. The anxiously attached two-year-old gets very upset when Dad or Mom leaves, refusing to be consoled by anyone or anything until they return. Even then, she clings and fusses for a very long time.

How it develops. As this child grows up, she often sees other people as her major source of security while viewing herself as weak, unworthy, or in danger if left alone. She may work hard to stay connected even if connection is hard. Healthy friendships may eventually help her become more secure and independent, but anxious or distant parents and friends may erode her confidence more. As an adult, she'll probably have a lot of worries and fears, including worry about wearing others out with all her worries and fears! She thinks her only choice is to do all she can to get other people's help, attention, and care. Sometimes that means getting angry, blaming, or controlling when she feels abandoned or afraid.

How might an anxious attachment style impact our relationship with God? Even when an anxiously attached adult really wants to be close to God, when that closeness wanes she may feel particularly abandoned or worthless. Because she feels unworthy and incapable on her own, she may beg and plead for God's help and protection, or work overtime to prove herself deserving of His care. If help doesn't show up in the form she desires, she may more readily feel rejected or think she's being punished. The deep gratitude and connection with God she feels at times may more readily dissolve into anxiety about whether God will be available enough.

+ Regardless of your attachment style, which of these characteristics or thoughts show up in your relationship with God, especially when you are under stress?

+ What event or problem, if anything, is currently making you feel insecure or anxious in your relationships or with God? Just naming these events or problems often helps us feel calmer and begin making plans to cope, so you might want to make a list of those challenges.

Style #2: Avoidant. The second of the less desirable attachment styles is avoidant attachment. Again, elements of this style may show up under stress even if you are generally more secure or have a different overall style. Take a look.

How it starts. This child may have experienced his parents' nurturing or support as inconsistent or absent, and he often feels actively ignored or criticized. As a toddler, he often ignores Mom or Dad even if they leave and seems indifferent when they return; however, his heart is actually pounding hard and his body shows silent signs of high stress. Although he looks strong or self-sufficient, this child may have more or less given up on his parents and often on people in general, no longer expecting them to be reliable sources of help or affection. He may also get angry quickly and for little obvious reason.

How it develops. As he grows up, the avoidantly attached adult usually sees himself as capable and others as weak, incompetent, or undependable. Under the surface, however, he harbors a lot of self-doubt and feels jealous and competitive with others. He often prides himself on being self-sufficient and independent and not having many needs, and he can develop a lot of skill, independence, and self-reliance. He might also distrust people and avoid closeness or commitment.

How might an avoidant attachment style impact our relationship with God? The avoidantly attached adult may not feel a real need for closeness with God, whether because he prides himself on independence or because he simply does not expect God to contribute much to his life. Emotional closeness is not something he necessarily values or seeks. In fact, it may make him anxious to get too close to another, even though he doesn't necessarily look anxious on the outside. He may also look down on religion as a kind of weakness, or be contemptuous of fellow church members who seem naïve or overly needy. Getting too close to others feels dangerous, but distancing leaves him alienated, lonely, and wondering about the real meaning of life.

Some people alternate between an anxious and an avoidant style, sometimes demanding and clinging, at other times retreating into frustrated or indifferent withdrawal. They may try to create hard-and-fast rules about how to relate to others, hoping the rules will simplify their confusion about how relationships work and what they can expect. Like those with the traumatic attachment style described below, they may have experienced a lot of chaos in their early years, or may have been forced to depend on people who also hurt them, leaving them with no reliable and safe way to get their needs for closeness met. We might expect them to vacillate with God as well, working hard at times to prove their worth and please God, but also expecting criticism or abandonment. They may find distance from God easier than closeness—or they may find distance almost intolerable. They may long for the magical quality religion had in childhood, when God felt like their only refuge in a stormy life.

+ What aspects of the avoidant attachment style resonate for you?

+ Under what circumstances are you most likely to avoid God?

Style #3: Traumatic. The final attachment style is traumatic attachment. If you experienced physical, verbal, emotional, or sexual abuse, or serious or ongoing neglect, chances are you'll have elements of this style. Early trauma—including extreme helplessness, isolation, or trauma inflicted by people you had to live with and depend on—is especially damaging to a long-term sense of stability and safety. Even though traumas like war, accidents, serious health problems, natural disasters, or civic violence are hard on anyone, they have a deeper impact on people who experienced trauma early in life.[6]

Note: If you've been traumatized, you may feel anxious, angry, or numb even reading this and being reminded of those experiences, whether or not you remember a lot of details about them. It may help to take a few minutes before you proceed to close your eyes, release tension in your body, and visualize a place where you feel safe and comfortable. Bring your awareness to where you are right now, reminding yourself that you are safe and in control in the present moment.

How it starts. Traumatically attached toddlers and children often see their parents or other adults as a source of threat or harm, even though they have no other place to turn for nurturing and care. They may be afraid and aggressive with other people, unusually manipulative, deceitful, or clingy, or they may appear to have given up on people almost entirely.

How it develops. As these children grow up, they may experience other people as untrustworthy, abusive, uncaring, and betraying. Their lingering hopes for emotional connection are often slim and tainted by rage, hatred, grief, humiliation, or numbness. They may lack empathy for others because little empathy has been shown to them. Their brains develop on high alert, so they could assume danger is lurking or abandonment likely at every turn. They tend to have an entrenched difficulty with trust. Protection, closeness, and caring are hard to "let in," but they also need these things to help soothe, calm, and heal them.

How might a traumatic attachment style impact our relationship with God? Some people with traumatic, neglectful, or isolating backgrounds do turn to God as the one trusted source of help in a painful world. Others consciously or unconsciously assume God is responsible for their pain, does not protect them, is indifferent to their suffering, and therefore cannot be trusted. In my experience as a therapist working with these clients, I have seen that it can be especially difficult for them to imagine that God grieves with them, has protected them in some ways they could not see, can redeem their traumatic experiences and turn them to learning and growth, or can help them find healing (greater peace and coping) even if they do not find a cure (becoming "like everyone else").

If you have a traumatic attachment style, practice listening to and caring for the part of you that is injured, alone, or afraid. Consider finding a therapist or counselor experienced in working with trauma. Look for a therapist who is comfortable working with spiritual issues as well, if possible. When counseling with ecclesiastical leaders, it may help to make them aware of your background.

- *What traumatic experiences, if any, have undermined your trust in people or God?*

Can We Change?

As we've noted already, there are probably many reasons children form more or less secure attachments with their parents.

Some children come into the world with bodies that are more difficult to soothe. Some parents struggle with their own attachment insecurities, with poverty and all the disruption it causes, or with other stressors that make it harder for them to read or meet their children's needs. Life circumstances of all kinds (such as illness, trauma, excessive change, or loss) can affect both parents' and children's ability to consistently bond and connect.

Unfortunately, our attachment style has significant impact on our developing brains regardless of how we got that way. People who are not securely attached not only have more anxiety or difficulty relating to others when they are young, but they take a different brain with them into adulthood. The parts of the brain that scan the environment for signs of threat are more active and developed, while their capacity for self-soothing is diminished. They are more likely to perceive threat in otherwise neutral settings. They are more likely to react strongly to threats they perceive. Ironically, sometimes they are more likely to put themselves in harm's way. All these tendencies tend to persist into adulthood, so the world and other people are likely to seem more unpredictable and chaotic, less manageable and inviting.[7]

Although new, more loving relationships can help people see options available to them now that were not available when they were young, I've noted with my clients that such relationships can be hard to come by when their early attachment experiences have left them prickly, clingy, or distant. They often have an intuitive sense that the unconditional, consistent love and understanding of another person could help them heal and change, so they may go looking for a spouse, a friend, or a God with such characteristics. They may think they have found just such a being, only to feel an enormous betrayal when they think the person or deity they chose has let them down. They may switch from seeing the other person as their rescuer and savior to seeing him or her as one more incarnation of the people who hurt them. Their disillusionment may arouse feelings of deep anger or despair that they assume are justified.[8]

Fortunately for all of us, even less secure children can become more secure adults as we get more conscious of our relationship predispositions, update those assumptions and expectations based on new understanding, and change what we tell ourselves our early experiences mean about us. But insight alone may not do the job. We may especially benefit from learning the self-soothing skills of meditation, empowering exercise or martial arts, creative experiences like theater or art, participation in like-minded groups, or individual therapy.[9]

Learning to tell the story of our early years with self-compassion and a broader perspective on our caregivers is another way of helping our attachment style to change. Turning a chaotic story into a sensible history can help (and we will explore how to do this in the next chapter). Through this process we can acquire what some attachment researchers call "earned secure attachment," which is a deeper sense of internal security than one would predict based on our life experience.[10] Even those of us who were not securely attached as children can gain the benefits of a more secure attachment style—including with God—as we come to a deeper and more conscious understanding of how we came to experience the world as we do. We are not just stuck with the level of development we acquired in childhood and adolescence. It is possible for us to continue to grow up throughout our lives.

Growing Up in God

It is pretty natural for us to do and become what we've seen and experienced with our parents, but it is not always helpful.

Christ told the Pharisees: "*I speak that which I have seen with my Father*: and *ye* do that which ye have seen with *your father*. . . . If God were your Father, ye would love me: for I proceeded forth and came from God" (John 8:38, 42).

Nevertheless, our early growing up amid the inevitable imperfections of our parents' lives is part of how we taste the bitter and learn to prize the good. In Moses 6:55 we read: "And the Lord spake unto Adam, saying: Inasmuch as thy children are conceived in sin, even so *when they begin to grow up*, sin conceiveth in their hearts, and they taste the bitter, that they may know to prize the good."

But our family is not our only home, nor is it our only opportunity to grow up. As we remember, relearn, and re-ground our relationship assumptions in a true understanding of who God is and how He feels about us, we are able to choose God as our Father and to grow up again—in Him. Joseph Smith prayed in the dedication of the Kirtland Temple:

> And do thou grant, Holy Father, that all those who shall worship in this house may be taught words of wisdom out of the best books, and that they may seek learning even by study, and also by faith, as thou hast said;
>
> And *that they may grow up in thee*, and receive a fulness of the Holy Ghost, and be organized according to thy laws, and be prepared to obtain every needful thing. (Doctrine and Covenants 109:14–15)

How can we grow up this second time? Some of the answers may be found in the verses just cited:

+ through "worship in [God's] house," where we can observe and experience the range of God's consistency and providence

- through being taught words of wisdom
- through study and faith
- through the gift of the Holy Ghost
- through organizing our lives according to God's laws

This kind of change can take much effort and patience, as we uproot ourselves from our mortal footings and choose instead to be rooted and grounded in God's love.

In the Book of Mormon, Jacob 5 provides an extended analogy that compares the house of Israel in various stages of apostasy and regeneration to a vineyard of growing trees. Sometimes the trees planted in the best spots of ground, perhaps like children in the best of families, do not bring forth good fruit. The reasons for this are not always clear. In contrast, the Lord of the vineyard notices that some of the trees in very poor parts of the vineyard (or in difficult family or life circumstances) sometimes bring forth sweet, plentiful fruit:

> And it came to pass that the Lord of the vineyard said unto his servant: Look hither; behold I have planted another branch of the tree also; and thou knowest that this spot of ground was poorer than the first. But, behold the tree. I have nourished it this long time, and it hath brought forth much fruit; therefore, gather it, and lay it up against the season, that I may preserve it unto mine own self. (Jacob 5:23)

It is so encouraging to me to realize that where we have been planted is not the primary indicator of how we will turn out, and that as we become "rooted and grounded in . . . the love of Christ, which passeth knowledge . . . [we] might [yet] be filled with all the fulness of God" (Ephesians 3:17, 19). Whether securely rooted in our previous relationships or not, we can work to become rooted and grounded in the love of Christ. In fact, sometimes our early deficits give us powerful motivation to come unto Christ and establish our identity in relationship with Him. However, we will need to practice deeper and deeper humility to truly let go of much of what we expect or assume about relationships based on our past experience in order to see God for who He really is.

Developing Humility

We do not immediately appreciate all the ramifications of having grown up in our families of origin, or how what we learned there may interfere with our ability to see, receive, and trust the Lord. We don't readily let go of conclusions we once came to about how to feel safe in an uncertain and dangerous world. It takes humility to acknowledge that some of what we currently believe about relationships, life, or a relationship with God may simply be wrong.

Humility (which is very different from shame) helps us have the courage to see that we are still following relationship rules we put together when we were but vulnerable children doing our imperfect and immature best to make sense out of life, and that we may unconsciously expect others to follow such rules as well, even if we don't like the result.

We may have to learn gradually to humbly pull ourselves away from our roots and reestablish ourselves in the True Vine. Jacob describes a process for regrafting the trees of a vineyard into good roots, clearing away the bad a little at a time as the tree becomes stronger. This process may also apply to us as we attempt to clear away assumptions we have drawn from difficult early experience with relationships—assumptions that are now limiting our ability to grow into the adults we want to be.

> And as they begin to grow ye shall clear away the
> branches which bring forth bitter fruit, according to the

strength of the good and the size thereof; and ye shall not clear away the bad thereof all at once, lest the roots thereof should be too strong for the graft, and the graft thereof shall perish, and I lose the trees of my vineyard. ... Wherefore ye shall clear away the bad according as the good shall grow, that the root and the top may be equal in strength, until the good shall overcome the bad. (Jacob 5:65–66)

Sometimes when we are in a power struggle with God, we really do simply need to repent. Sometimes when we feel distant from Him, we need to renew our efforts at scripture study, prayer, and service in order to shrink the distance between us. Sometimes when God feels far away, it is tempting to blame, cajole, retaliate, or withdraw from Him in turn as we try to get His attention. *But sometimes when God feels far away, neither our unworthiness nor His indifference is to blame.* We just have learned ways of relating that we need to unlearn if we are to grow up in God.

Some Questions

Sometimes there is nothing so helpful as a good question. Raymond learned a lot from his Sunday School teacher's question, and I have too. If you were to sum up who God is to you in one word, what would it be?

Are there other words that might come up for you at other times? Like what?

Is there an experience you've had that captures for you when you learned to see God this way?

As you think about your word, your image of God, do you think it is more:

- a hope? (as in, I hope God is this way but I don't really experience it)
- a truth? (as in, this word seems consistent with both the gospel and my experience)
- a lie? (as in, it feels like God is like this, but I don't think the all-good God would be this way)
- a misunderstanding? (as in, I was taught this, but it doesn't make sense to me)
- a temptation? (as in, this is what Satan wants me to believe, and I often take the bait)

Toxic Relationship Patterns and God

Four characteristics of marital relationships have been found to be so toxic, they help marital researchers predict with 91 percent accuracy which marriages will end in divorce.[11] While we all do some of these things some of the time, the more these patterns exist in a relationship, the harder it is for that relationship to survive. These toxic patterns show up in our relationship with God as well. They are:

- Criticism (pointing out the other person's weaknesses or faults)
- Contempt (name calling, eye rolling, head shaking, sarcasm, belittling)
- Defensiveness (denying responsibility and pushing blame back onto the other person)
- Stonewalling (refusing to talk about or bring up problems)[12]

The more we have seen and copied these patterns, the harder it is not to imagine that God is doing them too. When we imagine God being critical of our weaknesses, contemptuous of our faults, defending His own behavior while blaming us, or unwilling to engage with us, our relationship with Him will suffer. When we in turn are critical or contemptuous toward God, His Church, or His children, or when we are defensive or stonewall when He tries to help or correct us, it is difficult for us to feel His empathy and help.

So what helps couples better resolve differences and feel close despite incompatibilities? When couples can be *calm, curious, and compassionate* with themselves and their partners, especially at times of high stress or disagreement, they can generally work through their issues enough to feel genuine love and improvement in their marriage. These same qualities can help us with our children, bosses, friends, Church leaders . . . and with God. They provide a prescription for practicing humility.

It takes real humility to stop our tendencies to become defensive or blaming and to instead take a measured tone, to become genuinely curious about what we or another person thinks and feels, and to find compassion and a desire to help. When in times of stress or distance with God we can calm our worries with reminders of our reasons to believe, when we become curious about our own thoughts and feelings and the Lord's, and when we remain convinced of His genuine, humble compassion for us, we can be more humble and compassionate with ourselves.

Compassion for ourselves is much different from rationalization. Self-compassion makes our hearts soft and open and helps us find empathy for others, while rationalization makes us defensive and blaming. Self-compassion reminds us of our worth and motivates us to live our values, while shame locks us in to defensiveness and hiding. God may remind us of our values to inspire clarity and godly sorrow that lead to repentance, but He does not shame or humiliate us.[13]

Attaching to God

As we try to develop more trust in God, knowing our relationship predispositions—our attachment style and experience—can help. Christ can help us in our efforts to gain a secure bond with our Father, the Father toward whom Christ repeatedly points us. While it can be painful to accept that we may be the ones keeping God at a distance, there is also hope in this realization. If we are part of the problem, we can be part of the solution. Maybe God is not the punishing, disappointed, disinterested, or distant relational partner we have understood Him to be.

Of course, we will never have full control over a two-sided relationship, and God will have His own reasons for leaving us to struggle alone at times. Even the perfect Savior who said repeatedly, "the Father hath not left me alone; for I do always those things that please him" (John 8:29), also cried out, "My God, my God, why hast thou forsaken me?" (Matthew 27:46). But when we can humbly accept that the reasons for God's silence will never include indifference, powerlessness, or lack of empathy on His part, we can more humbly, patiently, and creatively endure, as we will continue to discuss in the next chapter.

(Note: See the Appendix for questions to help you further explore your attachment to God.)

Chapter 5

GAINING COMPASSION FOR THE PAST

Blessed is the man that trusteth in the Lord, and whose hope the Lord is. For he shall be as a tree planted by the waters, and that spreadeth out her roots by the river, and shall not see when heat cometh, but her leaf shall be green.

(Jeremiah 17:7–8)

Near Fish Lake in central Utah, a grove of quaking aspen trees proliferates what may be the oldest continuously living organism on our planet. Estimated to be 80,000 years old (and some claim as much as 1,000,000), this aspen grove predates by at least 70,000 years the last ice age, responsible for the creation of the Great Lakes. This "grove" of aspens is actually a single, male aspen tree with a massive underground root system that spreads across approximately 100 acres. What we see as individual aspen trees are merely stems growing off this single root, and all of the stems share a common genetic identity with the root. Even though individual stems are subject to forest fires, infestations, and climate changes, the root remains strong and prolific. This massive quaking aspen is named Pando, a Latin word meaning *I spread*.[1]

I can't imagine a more vivid incarnation of the principle Christ taught His disciples in the following scripture: "As the branch cannot bear fruit of itself, except it abide in the vine; no more can ye, except ye abide in me. I am the vine, ye are the branches: He that abideth in me, and I in him, the same bringeth forth much fruit: for without me ye can do nothing" (John 15:4–5).

We are as branches or stems growing from the enduring, unseen root or vine of Jesus Christ. That root gives us life, allowing us to continue to thrive through our mortal equivalents of both fire and ice. But unlike the aspen trees, our attachment to our Root is not merely an artifact of our existence. We must choose that attachment for it to continue to nourish us, sustain us, and allow us to bring forth fruit.

As discussed in the previous chapter, when we come into this world we are rooted and grounded first in a relationship with our earthly parents or caretakers—a relationship that may or may not foster feelings of security or understanding of our eternal relationship to God. Through gospel principles and temple ordinances, through our study of the wisdom found in the scriptures and the best books, through our faith and obedience to God's laws, we have the opportunity to grow up again—to grow up in God. He becomes the Father of our new development as we ponder, exercise faith, repent, change our minds about many things, and draw upon the empowering grace made available to us through the Atonement of Jesus Christ. As we do, we and our new families can become regrounded and re-rooted in the Living Christ. Our earthly relationships can heal, our capacity for charity and peace can expand, and our character can be honed and shaped to fit us for our promised land.

Although God allows all kinds of people to do all kinds of foolish things in this world, bringing us all sorts of heartaches, I am coming to believe that He will not allow anything to happen that He cannot fully and completely redeem to our benefit—if we so choose. His power to redeem all things and turn them to our learning and blessing is truly limitless. He is a genius at turning straw into gold.

Learning to trust, expect, and participate in that genius is a major aspect of our mortal experience. This is a simple idea that is not easy to remember or implement under duress. Perhaps this is an understanding that Paul wanted us to grasp when he prayed: "That Christ may dwell in your hearts by faith; that ye, being rooted and grounded in love, may be able to comprehend . . . the breadth, and length, and depth, and height [of] . . . the love of Christ, which passeth knowledge, that ye might be filled with all the fulness of God" (Ephesians 3:17–19).

As we model our prayers after the Lord's Prayer, the first line of which is, "Our Father which art in heaven, Hallowed be thy name," we root and ground ourselves again in this primal relationship with a loving Father. His name is hallowed or holy to us, which means that it is set apart from other names that are rooted and grounded in earthly things. We begin to look to Him instead of to earthly sources for our security, our identity, and our future possibilities.

When we call upon our Father in Heaven, we are reminded that in order to have a relationship with God unencumbered by our personal history with this fallen world, we must choose to hallow Him alone as our ultimate Father. Ironically, as we do so our relationships with our earthly parents and others often get deeper or clearer.

Looking Into Our Story

To help people better understand how expectations they learned as children might affect their assumptions about God, I have adapted an exercise developed for married couples to help people explore their relationship with God. I begin by asking them to remember some of the most positive traits of either of their parents or primary caretakers—traits like funny, hardworking, for-giving, warm, generous, flexible, bold, or responsible, and then to notice the traits that were most important to them personally. Next I invite them to remember some of the more negative traits of ei-ther of their parents as they experienced them as children—things like their parents being critical, absent, dishonest, depressed, dan-gerous, boring, stingy, or intrusive, and to notice which traits were most troublesome. I also ask them to recall some of the things they feared as they interacted with their parents, and they sometimes note things like fear of being neglected, embarrassed, rejected, abandoned, used, or hurt. Finally, I invite them to think about what they wanted most from their parents but didn't get, like an apol-ogy, an explanation, safety, acceptance, to feel important, or to feel loved. You might reflect on these questions as well. (If you'd like to do this exercise yourself, you'll find it and two others under the Chapter 5 subheading in the Appendix.)

Next, I invite the people to consider how these old experiences might impact their relationship with God. Children tend to see their parents in somewhat black-and-white terms, and those con-clusions and emotions run quite deep. As a result, many of us un-consciously spend our lives searching for a God with the positive traits we most valued in our parents, but we also unconsciously both look for and fear evidences that God is really more like the negative traits we experienced as children. We may unconsciously expect God to make us feel those things we feared in our inter-actions with our parents. And when we have those feelings, we wish God would give us what we most wanted but did not get as children . . . even though unconsciously we don't think He will. The negative thoughts and feelings we had repeatedly about our-selves as children (feelings like worry, frustration, fear, shame, or abandonment) can also come up in our relationship with God, especially when we are under stress or our needs are not met, and we may assume God is responsible for making us feel this way. We may respond to God in a grown-up version of the ways we typically responded to frustration as children, such as by arguing, sneaking around, walking out, complaining to others, feeling sorry for ourselves, or having a tantrum. Yet what we need to do to grow is often the opposite of whatever we used to do. We may need to try listening instead of arguing, coming out into the open instead of sneaking, trying harder instead of quitting, looking for good instead of complaining, building gratitude instead of self-pity, or calming ourselves with relaxation and meditation instead of working ourselves into a tantrum.

Our goal in thinking about our childhood frustrations or fears is not to blame our parents, but to look at the ways in which our adult responses to life may still be affected by conclusions (often shortsighted or limited in perspective) that we came to as children. Just writing these things down can help us tell a piece of our story. And telling our story, it turns out, helps us change it.

Rewriting Our Story

Even when our attachment history is troubled, we don't have to pass on a negative attachment style to our children. We can "earn" a more secure attachment style if we didn't come by one naturally.[2] We don't do this by working really, really hard to be good, so don't get too panicked about that word *earn*. We do it by rethinking our stories to add elements that make them more coherent, self-reflective, objective, and flexible. In a sense, we learn to turn our personal story into history.

How does a history differ from a story? When I tell a story from my life I recount the events I remember. The story may trigger strong emotions as I re-experience its impact, or I may block off intense emotions I couldn't handle and have not really made sense of. I see the story primarily from my personal perspective, so it may be difficult to grasp the perspectives of others. Likewise, I may not have a clear sense of how the story fits in with the rest of my life, what options I had, who was affected by it and how, or what I truly need in order to redeem what happened and turn it to good.

History is a little different. When people write history they certainly tell stories, but they set those stories in a context of broader themes and trends. They include the perspectives, motives, cultures, and personalities of many people. They look at antecedents and consequences of individual events to see larger patterns and lessons. To be sure, they describe the emotional impact of events on people, and when we read history our emotions can certainly be aroused, but emotions are interwoven with more understanding than is commonly available to any one person feeling his or her way through a personal story. We may come away from a story feeling great empathy for an individual; we come away from history with a bigger picture of how stories from many sources fit together and impact each other.

When we can learn to make sense of our own stories in a similar way, we too gain a broader perspective on what happened to us. We are able to see the points of view of others more compassionately and completely. The antecedents and consequences of events begin to make more sense. Lessons we took from the story get clearer. We begin to imagine choices we could not see or maybe did not have at the time—choices we might use in the future. The story feels less chaotic and emotionally intense. We can see more clearly what is really going on, not just our own piece of it or a small moment of it. We can come to different conclusions about what it means to us and our future.

Changing Story to History

As we gain some insights into the ways our childhood story shapes how we experience God, we hopefully see some new options for how we might experience that relationship differently. We may begin to understand better why we are stuck in the past, closed off to the real God, who stands ready to heal, love, and teach us. As we come to see our history and the broader implications of our story, we climb out of our emotional reactions and faulty conclusions of the past and move toward the perspective of God, which He describes here:

> Thus saith the Lord your God, even Jesus Christ, the Great I Am, Alpha and Omega, the beginning and the end, the same which looked upon the wide expanse of eternity, and all the seraphic hosts of heaven, before the world was made;
>
> The same which knoweth all things, for all things are present before mine eyes. (Doctrine and Covenants 38:1–2)
>
> All things . . . past, present, and future . . . are continually before the Lord. (Doctrine and Covenants 130:7)

Because God sees the past, the present, and the future as an integrated whole, He knows how any single story fits into the larger context of who we are becoming, what we are learning, and what we can contribute now and in eternity to the furthering of His work and glory. He hears our protestations, coming out of our tiny slice of our story, when we do not trust Him or we fear He is not on our side; however, He always sees the bigger picture and can gradually help us to see it as well.

A sweet friend of mine who has undergone extensive and difficult challenges of all sorts, and who has nevertheless worked very hard to grow in her faith and resilience through them, found herself confronted with yet another frightening and serious setback. She wanted to believe that the Lord would help her, but that help did not seem to be forthcoming. She prayed with some desperation, "Heavenly Father, I'm trying so hard to trust you. Please don't let me down." The answer formed quickly and clearly in her mind, "Daughter, I'm not trying to trust you. I do trust you. You can do this. I will help you."

Lessons my friend has learned in recent years about trusting God compete with her early stories of betrayal and abandonment. She has already learned from her own story to feel a deep empathy with others who suffer. Now God is teaching her to add to her story a deeper trust in herself and in God. This combination of compassion for self and others and trust in God creates deep wisdom and courage in the face of life's tragedies. It makes her a powerful instrument in both helping others and holding onto peace and hope. She is turning isolated stories into a comprehensive history that includes these new lessons.

What Can You See?

In the next ninety days (or shall we make that ninety minutes?) you are likely to face some experience that threatens your feelings of safety in the world. Depending on your attachment style, you may be particularly sensitive to experiences that make you feel insecure around other people, that undermine your self-image, that overwhelm your capacities, that you aren't motivated to tackle even though you need to, that evoke feelings of anger or depression or fear, that make you feel rejected, or that you simply don't know how to handle.

When those things happen, it will be hard to remember that your assessment of that situation reflects what you've learned to

perceive and expect, not necessarily what is. The fear you feel today may belong to the past; it may not reflect the actual level of
threat in the present. Anger you feel now may be motivated by old
injustices more than current ones. Your current sadness may be
compounded by prior losses not yet fully understood or mourned.
These prior experiences and recurring emotions can make it difficult to see God's protection, kindness, or guidance now. What's
more, we are likely to use the same tools and tricks we've learned in
the past to try to engage God today. We may manipulate Him for
what we want as we tried to manipulate our parents, use outdated
tools to cope with new relationship challenges, or predict responses
from God based on we've seen in others before. What really is going on and how we can best respond to meet our needs can be quite
different from what comes naturally.

In the interest of (sort of) full disclosure, let me just say that
my run through the exercise mentioned above produced the following picture of my own relationship with God:

I have spent my life looking for a God who enjoys me, provides for me, and is involved with me, even though I unconsciously
look for and fear evidences that God is really critical, distant, and
preoccupied with more important concerns. Without fully realizing it, I expect God to be disappointed in me, and then I wish He
would only listen without having to be right, or that He would go
someplace else and take care of His own problems, even though I
don't think He will. When I'm under stress or my needs are not
met, I often feel ignored, dominated, or like I can't keep up, and I
assume God is responsible for my feelings. Then I often respond
by resisting, blaming myself, taking care of others and ignoring
what I need, or trying to get around what is expected. What I
really need to do instead is the opposite of that—which would be
to (1) ask more directly for what I need from others and from the

Lord, (2) express compassion and empathy for myself, (3) be open to receiving compassion and empathy from God, and (4) take risks to work consistently, creatively, and cheerfully on the challenge at hand. I need to do these things while "trusting my all to Thy tender care, and knowing Thou lovest me."[3]

Granted, the latter are not skills I would expect myself (or anyone) to have had as a child, which is when I acquired my worldview. These options were not available to me then. I did about the best I could with what I had. So did you. And so did our parents, friends, and spouses. But our current stressors can put us back into a part of our brain that still operates on old assumptions about how the world works and what we can expect from ourselves, other people, and the Lord.

The good news is that brains can change. If I can recognize these old assumptions more consciously, I can begin to train my brain to scan for different kinds of evidence than what I'm used to focusing on. For example, brain research supports that making a list every day of three new things I'm grateful for helps retrain my brain to see blessings, not just threats. Exercising daily reminds my brain that I can choose power over passivity. Meditation helps my brain slow down and self-soothe. Taking creative risks and tackling problems create new neuronal connections in my brain that make me smarter and more optimistic.

These changes in my brain also help me notice the ways God supports, rescues, and teaches me (not just the ways He doesn't). I more readily tackle life's inevitable problems, assuming I agreed in the premortal world to take on certain challenges that can teach me things I wanted then to learn, help me contribute, and allow me to complete a mission I signed up for. I begin to see choices I make to keep God far away, and how to make other choices instead.

And when I fail to accomplish these lofty goals, disintegrating instead into the hopelessness, frustration, or self-absorption that come more naturally, I can regroup and try again, assured that God is all the things He invites me to become: long-suffering, gentle, meek, loving, kind, wise, faithful, charitable, righteous, humble, guileless, and without any desire to exercise compulsion upon my soul (see Doctrine and Covenants 121:37–46). In short, He is not my enemy, but my constant and compassionate companion.

Like you, I didn't just come here to learn from other people's heartaches, losses, and failures, but by my own experience. That means I've had experiences with abuse and trauma God didn't protect me from, prayers that God didn't answer in any way I could identify, failures and serious mistakes God didn't let me see coming in time to prevent, injuries God hasn't yet healed, and losses God didn't restore or avert. Such experiences come to all that they may "know good from evil; wherefore they are agents unto themselves" (Moses 6:56). We get to choose whether we will learn from our experience to be bitter, afraid, and resentful, or compassionate, nonjudgmental, and patient. We get to choose charity, or one of its many antitheses: indifference, blame, shame, pride, jealousy, and fear.

Developing Compassion

When you are hurting, how do your thoughts about who God really is differ from what you believe when things are going fine? Are you more likely to feel angry, distant, betrayed, or afraid? What would it feel like to acknowledge you came to these conclusions honestly, that God has great empathy with you in all of them, and that even when they are unhelpful or limiting or inaccurate, He understands?

I got a chance to find out my own reactions when my husband and I were writing a book a few years ago. This was a particularly challenging project for me, for a lot of reasons. One Saturday, a deadline looming, I spent a long, hard day writing and rewriting a particular chapter that needed serious reworking. I worked for hours, tackling one problem at a time. I think I truly gave it all I had. Finally satisfied, I saved the file as I heard my oldest daughter come in through the back door for our planned outing to the general Relief Society meeting broadcast at the stake center. I felt enormous relief to have this chapter completed and to be able to now take a needed and uplifting break.

As I gathered my purse and coat to leave, I remembered a small additional detail I needed to add to the chapter, so I quickly returned to the computer to open the file. To my absolute horror, none of the work I had done all day had saved. It had all mysteriously disappeared into cyberspace. I had no idea where it had gone. I frantically tried everything I could think of to recover my edits, to no avail. I don't know how to describe the panic I felt. I could not begin to imagine how I would possibly re-create the work I had done, nor did I have time to. I did not just pray. I pleaded and begged and pounded on the door of heaven asking God to help me find this file. Nothing.

I finally encouraged my daughter to go to the meeting without me, knowing that I was too upset to get anything out of it and that if I didn't find this file soon I was going to be up all night and would need every spare minute to try to re-create the work I had lost. In addition to praying, I emailed the computer specialist at my husband's work. I got online and looked up possible solutions. I paid some computer expert on a website to help me. I called other people I knew who are especially tech-savvy. Everyone was very sympathetic with my distress. Everybody had suggestions. Nobody was able to help me. The file was simply, inexplicably gone. I almost felt physically ill.

I remember where I was standing as I tried to calm myself

down enough to truly and submissively pray. I remember feeling sort of ashamed for being this upset about a lousy computer file when there were so many problems in the world that were far, far more serious and horrific. But as I sent my prayers off toward heaven, I heard again the words I'd heard years before:

Why do you keep me so far away?

Once again, I was holding God at a distance, even as I thought I was inviting Him near.

I sat down on the couch, regrouped, and asked God to sit right next to me where I could feel His comforting presence. I tried really hard to compose myself enough to tell the Lord that as much as I wanted this problem fixed, if fixing it wasn't an option for some reason, then I trusted that He could still redeem this loss. I tried so hard to practice the faith I have often felt that God won't allow anything to happen to us that He cannot use for good. I tried to imagine possibilities for how that might occur. Perhaps He could give me the energy to do the rewrite again. Perhaps He could even help me make it better the next time. Perhaps I could learn a lesson in patience, empathy, or humility that would bless me. I asked Him with all the faith I could muster to just help me feel that He was sitting with me and would not leave me comfortless.

Now, I've displayed far less dignified responses to the inconveniences of life that I think God should spare me, but this time I knew hysterics were not called for or helpful. I was still *really* upset, but amid all my angst, I really didn't want to make a mountain out of what I knew was really a molehill in the landscape of human problems. Nevertheless, it took everything I had to hold on to some semblance of genuine humility and trust in the Lord instead of drowning in anger or self-pity.

Remarkably, as I sat on the couch and reached for God, I felt some angel of His presence near (see Isaiah 63:9). To my astonishment, this Being never communicated, "Wendy, really, do you know what life is like for people in Sierra Leone? Do you know how many people lost loved ones today? You lost a computer file. Really. Grow up." In fact, what I felt Him saying to me, and mean it, was, "Yes, this is really hard. I completely understand. You worked really hard on this, and you're really frustrated. I get it."

And it was that compassion, that charity, that nonjudgmental acceptance of my feelings and limitations that changed everything. I realized that the shame I had felt, all wrapped up in my frustration with my incompetence at both computers and resilience, was actually worse than the loss itself. When I realized He didn't think I needed to be ashamed, the loss felt more tolerable. Perhaps I really could grow up and take this like an adult. In feeling Him join me in my human frustration, I felt like I could join Him in His godly perspective.

I went back to my office, pulled out my scriptures, and asked God to help me find solace in them until I could calm down enough to concentrate on my long editing task. As I read, I learned something sweet and helpful, my heart calmed, and I began to prepare emotionally to redo the chapter. Only then did the computer expert at my husband's work call me back, having just gotten my email and somehow, miraculously even to him, retrieved the lost file.

Things don't always turn out this way, of course. God cannot, or at least does not, make up all our losses so quickly. But I learned a powerful lesson. God's compassion and charity were what helped me cope with this loss—not frantic efforts to convince God that I couldn't handle it, not shame about not handling it better, not anger, self-pity, or blame. Christ's compassionate empathy for my plight and His charitable but nonpatronizing acceptance of my frustration helped me feel a compassionate but nonpatronizing self-acceptance, and *that* gave me the clarity and courage to change course.

Seeing Beyond the Veil

The more we understand our past, the more options God can help us imagine for our future. Occasionally the vistas He opens up to us extend beyond this life. I am fascinated by the experiences some people have had with life beyond the veil. Almost universally, people who have seen that other world lose their fear of death, become preoccupied with love and learning, and experience a kind of healing and peace unfamiliar to them here. They can also find it enormously difficult to stay in mortality after such an experience, and they are often filled with longing to return home. I have enough of that longing already, so perhaps it is just as well that I don't have experiences that would intensify it before it is my time to leave. But I am grateful that there are at least a few people strong enough to come back and tell us that God can truly redeem and heal all of our mortal suffering, turning it to our eternal learning and growth.

I am also grateful for those who have not been given such visions, but who still have been given such lessons. One Holocaust survivor was often told by friends, "I cannot believe in a God who allows such things to happen." Her response was simply, "That is the only God there is." Poignantly, we either open our hearts to this God for companionship in surviving, learning from, healing from, and preventing such catastrophes in the future, or we succumb to the devastating illusion that we are utterly alone with disastrous and pointless outcomes of our own and others' agency. Even Christ, the perfect one, felt that utter aloneness at least once as He languished on the cross, and we will surely feel it as well. But He was *not* alone.

And we are not alone. Nor are we indelibly shaped by the ways we've grown up in the past. We are offspring of a loving Father, who is in heaven, whose name we hallow, and who sees the end from the beginning. With His help, we can grow up in God.

Chapter 6

CHOOSING TRUST
FOR THE FUTURE

—◦◦◦✚◦◦—

Fear not, I am with thee; oh, be not dismayed,
For I am thy God and will still give thee aid.
I'll strengthen thee, help thee, and cause thee to stand,
Upheld by my righteous, omnipotent hand.
("How Firm a Foundation," Hymns, no. 85)

After invoking the hallowed name of our Father in Heaven, the Lord's Prayer petitions, "Thy kingdom come. Thy will be done in earth, as it is in heaven" (Matthew 6:10).

What might be going on in your life if you were to find yourself praying, "Thy will be done?" What feelings does that phrase evoke for you? I recently asked a number of people those questions. Here are some of their responses (names have been changed):

> I might be reluctant to pray "Thy will be done" because I'm afraid of what His will might actually be. —Clark

> Initially there is a wrestle. Something is going on in my life that I can't control the outcome to, but I *desperately want to.* I try on all the "what if" scenarios over and over to the point of exhaustion. —Rebecca

> Saying it is one thing, but meaning it requires delving to the core of my being and letting go of my limited sense of identity and shortsighted plans. It means *totally* trusting

that He sees who I really am, who I can potentially become, and the paths I should walk in that process. —Antonia

Usually if I'm praying "Thy will be done," I'm anticipating having to make a sacrifice of some kind, or someone I love is going to get hurt and there's nothing I can do to stop it, or I'm being asked to do an unpleasant chore from God. I associate those words with grief, pain, and powerlessness. I find this very unfortunate, because I *want* to believe that God's will for my life is to fill it with joy, light, truth, and peace. But I find myself avoiding "God's will" for fear that unity with Him will require painful sacrifice that will drain my resources and leave me feeling depleted and alone. —Cathy

Then I asked them how they felt about God's kingdom coming. They said:

It will be great once God's kingdom actually gets here, but it is a little scary to think about everything that has to happen before that day comes. —Caroline

If I am there to see it, either as a mortal caught up or a spirit brought back, then I will be thrilled. It is that nagging "if" that introduces just enough anxiety to my thoughts to make me realize I have a long way to go. —Patricia

God's kingdom coming to the earth can't come fast enough. I am frightened to raise children in a world moving towards greater wickedness. —Kent

I am not one who is waiting for God's kingdom to return to the planet. I am not sure which God would show up: a vengeful, punitive, bigoted, rules-for-no-reason God, or the God of all-encompassing love that most people who have had near-death experiences describe. I'm also not sure what His administration would look like—some of His minions here on earth have been pretty harsh. Makes me nervous to think about it. —Angela

While it seems like a very nice thing to pray for God's will to be done and His kingdom to come, those words can also bring up our fear of what the future holds, what kind of a God is actually running the world, and what God may require of those who call themselves disciples. Such hesitations and fears can make us reluctant to let God close.

The LDS Bible Dictionary reminds us, "The first effect of Adam's sin was that he was afraid (Gen. 3:10). Sin destroys that feeling of confidence God's child should feel in a loving Father and produces instead a feeling of shame and guilt. Ever since the Fall God has been teaching men not to fear, but with penitence to ask forgiveness in full confidence of receiving it."[1]

Unfortunately, sinning is not the only human experience that can cause us to fear God or lose confidence in Him.

The Impact of the Past on Our View of the Future

We've talked about how our attachment patterns can influence how we approach or imagine God. If you felt secure and safe in your early years, and the people who raised you were compassionate, consistent, and competent at helping you manage life, you have a better chance of looking toward the future with optimism and confidence. And you have a better chance of feeling trust and hope when you imagine God's will being done.

There are also many reasons why you might not come by such trust naturally, however. Some children come into this world with a predisposition to anxiety even before life happens to them. Others have an attachment history that encourages and trains them in anxiety, making it much more challenging to remain calm and much easier to feel threatened. Early experiences with trauma and loss also program the brain to stay on high alert even after the danger is past. Once that background gets activated, we get more vigilant for signs of threat, we interpret ambiguous data more negatively, we get defensive more easily, and we react to later trauma more strongly and lastingly than other people. This also happens in our relationship with God.

We lived to tell the tale of threats we've survived because we didn't forget what corner they were lurking around. Our brains are still working hard to remember and prevent those dangers. Social dangers (shame, abandonment, rejection, betrayal) are recorded in the same region of the brain as physical threats. In other words, people are not just afraid of death, disease, and dismemberment. We're also afraid of abandonment, bullying, contempt, disapproval, and the rest of the alphabet of social threats to our safety and well-being. In fact, just being around an authority figure, having to interact with strangers, encountering novelty of any kind, or receiving negative feedback can trigger feelings of threat and defensiveness. And the less securely attached we feel, the more energy we must devote to:

- Scanning for threats
- Trying to decide what potential threats really mean (draining brain energy away from more creative, life-enhancing tasks)
- Preparing to fight or flee (then having to metabolize all the adrenaline we've produced regardless of whether the threat was real or imagined)
- Making excuses for our behavior (out of fear that others will judge or reject us unless we produce some reasonable excuse)
- Boosting our self-esteem artificially (by competing with or criticizing others)

As I perceive and respond to threat, I don't have to be faster than the proverbial bear; I just have to be faster than *you* so you'll be the one to get eaten, picked on, shamed, or beaten out in a competition instead of me. You become my enemy as well as the bear, and soon my whole world seems full of predators. My perception of the world as a dangerous place escalates.

In contrast, when we feel more securely attached:

+ We more readily feel compassion for ourselves rather than shame or self-pity, leading us to hide less and take more responsibility for our behavior.
+ We can also feel compassion for others in distress—rather than feeling so distressed by their distress that we have to take care of ourselves instead of them.
+ We are more likely to help and care for others even if there is no personal gain, making us more genuinely altruistic.
+ We can focus on how in this moment we are safe and secure enough, allowing our brain and body to truly rest.
+ We notice that we are lovable and important to others, and that we also care about them.
+ We feel free to be curious rather than rigid in how we see the world and other people.
+ We see ourselves as both competent and open to learning more, leading to increased confidence.

It isn't too hard to figure out that feeling securely connected to others also helps us feel safer with the Lord, which in turn makes the world feel like a more trustworthy place. By contrast, insecure attachments diminish our feelings of safety in the world and make it harder for us to trust the God who put us here.

Rachel is a talented and capable professional and an attentive wife and mother, but Rachel grew up in an environment of harshness, abuse, and loss. At least in part because her early family life was more frightening than supportive, her early experience with religion was also more frightening than supportive. As a child she was on the lookout for signs of impending danger from her angry and intense father, or for signs of disdain or indifference from her mother. That hypervigilance also meant she noticed, remembered, and could vividly imagine anything anxiety-provoking she heard about God. Those images persisted into adulthood, long after her conversion to the LDS faith. She writes:

> The moment I think "God," there is a *huge*, powerful image of God standing above me, looking down. He is tall, thin, and bony with a menacing face, and before I ever see the face, I see a huge mass of black with a big gold cross splashed across it, and He has a clipboard and pencil and is looking down at me just waiting for me to sin.
>
> I also have a memory of the nuns telling us that the job of the angels is to restrain God from acting in His fury to destroy us for sinning. So I have this picture of this huge, tall, black, menacing creature straining forward over me and being literally held back by legions of angels because *His* aim would be to destroy me, as in raining down fire or machetes to slice me to pieces. This is constant. It's always there.
>
> The nuns told us that God allows the angels to restrain Him to give us every opportunity to clean up our lives and stop sinning so as to lessen our time in purgatory where we'll be burning to pay for our sins. And the image of burning was very clear: literally set on fire. The pain of hell is that we will be continually burning—set on fire without ever being consumed—while in purgatory we're also going to be set on fire but at some point God will say that it's enough and now we can come into heaven. Where we will be disembodied and float around praising God, with

no relationships with anyone. From time to time, a spirit that seems familiar may pass by us, but the only kind of interaction in heaven is of us praising God who continues to sneer at us.

Prayer is always accompanied by a *strong* skepticism that God has any interest at all in anything I'm saying, and feeling that my words are something He gives only slight attention to, if any at all. I pray because I've been commanded to pray. I have so little genuine belief that my prayers are efficacious or anything other than an irritation to Him.

It just continues to astound me that people I associate with have this image of God as a loving Being who lives to bless their lives and share His goodness with them—a Protector, a Confidant, someone safe. If I am ever able to get to that image, it will only be after wading through this constant, continuing minefield.[2]

It isn't hard to imagine how Rachel might feel about uttering the words, "Thy will be done, Thy kingdom come." Although her worldview has evolved in many ways as she has matured in the gospel, her powerfully engrained childhood view of God sits deep in the trunk of her personal theological tree, influencing everything that grows out of it. She has spent a lot of years in both the Power Struggle and Withdrawal Stages of relationship with God.

The Catholicism Rachel remembers from childhood does not accurately represent Catholicism today. In any case, people from every faith tradition, including Mormonism, can develop conscious or unconscious views of God that make it hard for them to trust Him. Those childhood conclusions about God persist, even when our conscious mind believes God to be loving and benevolent.

Rachel has worked hard over decades to challenge and replace her lingering images of how she thinks God feels about her and to tame the anxiety that crashes through her calm, confident exterior when her brain perceives a threat. But it hasn't been easy for her to see the evidences of God's love, protection, or tender care. When hard things happen to her, as they do to all of us, her mind and body go on such high alert that all she can think of is how to placate and soothe the savage beast that is her image of God. She cannot anticipate His kingdom or the path to it with anything but dread. The future looks bleak indeed.

Are We Just Asking for Trouble?

Rachel isn't alone. Helen had a much more positive upbringing, but she still writes, "I really want to feel closer to the Lord, but sometimes I'm almost afraid to try. It's my understanding that when we have a spiritual experience, God tests us accordingly, and I've got enough tests without asking for more. Look what happened to Abraham!"

I can relate to that fear. I too was taught that Satan gets especially interested in us when we are trying to be good, or when we have a powerful spiritual experience. I also heard those ironic comments in Sunday School classes that "we all know what happens when you pray for patience or humility," which is supposedly that God will then try your patience and not only humble but humiliate you.

But I'm becoming less and less convinced that desiring to be close to God is "just asking for trouble." Mortality tests and tries us all. We notice these tests more when we see their contrast with sweet spiritual experiences or when we recognize our need for patience or humility, just like we suddenly notice a vocabulary word we just learned popping up everywhere, or a car model we just bought suddenly hogging every road. Drawing close to the Spirit doesn't prevent problems, to be sure, but I don't think it invites problems, either. What drawing close to God does do is qualify us to obtain spiritual help in turning *inevitable and universal* experiences with suffering, temptation, and difficulty into learning and growth.

As for Abraham—his story actually fills me with hope because Abraham didn't start out with some amazing legacy of secure and safe attachment. In fact, Abraham's own father sought his life, giving us some clues about the attachment issues with which Abraham may have contended. Yes, he had some unusual experiences and challenges. But let's not forget that Abraham didn't lose his son just because he dared to follow God. In fact, Abraham didn't lose his son at all. Actually, Abraham and two of his children were all rescued by angelic intervention. Abraham obtained unprecedented promises and blessings from God for himself and his posterity. Abraham and his sons, grandsons, and great-grandsons lived long and successful lives, learned to deeply trust the Lord, and became great patriarchs whose spiritual blessings still unfold upon their children through countless generations.

Although children sometimes suffer or die in this world, God doesn't look around to find who is trying to get close to Him and take their children as a test of their faith. That is not the God I have come to love and trust. I find comfort in God's tender words to Abraham as God rescues him from those who seek his life:

> Abraham, Abraham, behold my name is Jehovah, and I have heard thee, and have come down to deliver thee, and to take thee away from thy father's house, and from all thy kinsfolk . . . because they have turned their hearts away from me. . . . Behold, I will lead thee by my hand, and I will take thee, to put upon thee my name . . . and my power shall be over thee. (Abraham 1:16–18)

Abraham was not spared all trials or heartaches any more than we are, but God certainly blessed him on his way.

When we look at the entire history of the world and society, let alone when we ponder eternity, the wicked and spiritually apathetic certainly suffer more than those seeking God do. Addictions, defenses, unbridled passions, and disobedience to God's commandments may provide a temporary relief or escape from life's challenges, but they hardly protect us from or prepare us for the next round of life's inevitable challenges. In fact, they expose us to additional problems: they prevent the growth and maturing we need to soothe our troubled emotions, creatively solve our problems, deepen our compassion and self-compassion, and grow up in God. Drawing closer to the Lord doesn't set us up for problems. It strengthens our resilience, allowing us to find peace even when we cannot change our circumstances.

God cannot teach us what we need to know by only giving life's hardest puzzles to someone else, however. Growing up in God requires us to relinquish the false hope for permanent safety and protection. We all came on purpose to a fallen world full of challenges and losses. Of all the names for Christ in the scriptures, and there are dozens, He is never called the Preventer. Satan is the one who pretends he can keep us safe from trouble or fear, but his techniques for preserving our safety include enticing us to betray those we love, give in to out-of-control emotions, and succumb to poor judgment, despair, and sin. The false hope that God will change other people for our benefit, coddle us in sin, or protect us from loss and difficulty inevitably fails, as do self-pity, rage, or avoidance of spiritual work.

So if we can't count on God to always protect or rescue us, what can we count on Him for? Abraham's story implies that we can count on God to send angels, seen or unseen, to strengthen and help us and our children. We can count on God to respond to our pleas according to a wisdom greater than ours. We can count on God to help us find meaning and growth through our challenges. We can count on God to help us develop compassion, courage, humility, and faith when darkness reigns or losses multiply. We can count on God for endless posterity, priesthood power, and sustenance sufficient for our needs. In short, we can count on God to redeem every heartache He allows to come our way and to use it to bless us—if we will let Him.

What can we do to bring the blessings of Abraham, Isaac, and Jacob into our lives, even though we will also have trials and heartaches? Let's consider six practical ways to increase our security and trust in the God of Abraham. These tools are based on things I've learned from Rachel and others, from research on developing secure attachment, and from my own experience with wrestling with God for His promises to be fulfilled.

Learning to Trust the God of Abraham, Step One: Examine and Rethink Your Image of God

Stop for a few minutes and think about God and about how it feels to approach Him in prayer. Notice what comes up for you. You can reflect on the last time you prayed (or thought about praying), or you can pray now and see how it feels. You may have a visual image of God, a vague impression, an emotional response, a hunch, or you may not have anything come up at all. Just see.

As you imagine God, you might also consider the following questions:

+ When you prepare to pray, where do you visualize God being?
+ Where would you like Him to be? Is that possible? Why or why not? Are you sure?

- In your mind, what is He like? What is He doing? What is He thinking?
- What is the look on His face? What does His body language communicate?
- Is anyone else with Him? If so, what are they doing? If not, why not?
- What do you want Him to do? What do you need Him to understand?
- How does He respond to you? How do you feel about His response?

Whatever comes up for you, honor it. If the image is positive and encouraging, receive it and hold it gently and gratefully. If the image is troubling, receive that and hold it gently and gratefully as well. But also wonder about it. Where might these images have come from, and what might they teach you about where you can learn or grow?

How you envision God may be spot-on or wildly off from who He really is or what you more consciously believe. But once you know what images you bring to prayer, you can more consciously focus on your deepest beliefs and experiences with the Spirit instead of on images that evoke fear or doubt. Make sure to be compassionate with the part of you that holds images that interfere with your faith, however. Shame and blame don't help. What does the part of you that is distrustful, angry, or resistant to God need the rest of you to understand?

Learning to Trust the God of Abraham, Step Two: Practice Reminders of Secure Attachments

None of us can tolerate feeling detached for long. When we feel disconnected and alone, our attachment style gets activated quickly, prompting us to take whatever action we learned in the past to do when we needed to get reconnected. For some of us, that means appropriately asking for help and support, inviting a friend to lunch, or trustingly telling God about our problem. For others it may entail whining, self-pity, rage, icy withdrawal, acting out on an addiction, threatening to leave, or despair. Even if we've generally outgrown these unhelpful bids for connection, they can come back with a vengeance when we feel overstressed and alone. Brad writes:

> I was on a business trip recently and I felt really alone with a big project, and the next thing I know I'm acting like this big martyr, mad at God about all I have to do and never getting any help. But I feel nothing. God just sits there like He doesn't care at all. Then I start pulling away, I guess hoping God will notice and come after me and give me some help. I know in my head that God cares about me, but sometimes it is sure hard to feel it. But I don't like getting so upset.[3]

Regularly boosting feelings of attachment security helps people feel safer, more resilient, and more willing to take the risks required to grow.

Below is a list of activities that helped people in various research studies to feel more securely attached, positively affecting their subsequent performance, feelings, or relationships. These activities can boost our general feelings of safety and security and help us feel more willing to explore, try hard, and take risks. When we feel more safely connected to those we love and rely on, we are less likely to feel desperate with God. I've also added in italics some ways to explicitly apply each idea to our relationship with God and to directly feel closer to Him. These activities prepare our brain to see and receive evidences of our secure connection to loved ones and to God, and to strengthen our capacity for resilience.

1. Women in one research study endured a painful, frightening procedure with less stress and discomfort when they could touch the hand of their spouse.[4] To strengthen feelings of secure attachment, go straight for physical closeness to those you rely on. Call, schedule a visit, or just walk over and touch or hug someone you love. *With God, strengthen feelings of physical closeness by going to the temple or the temple grounds, walking in nature, looking at the stars, or imagining God sitting close to you. Tune in to physical feelings that accompany feeling the Spirit for you (like feelings of warmth, intensity, or aliveness).*

2. Just remembering the names and faces of loved ones helped people in another study feel calmer and more willing to endure pain.[5] *Prime your attachment security with God by reading through names of Christ in the Bible Dictionary or looking at artwork that helps you visualize the loving face of the Savior. Remember Christ is your Advocate with the Father, to whom we pray in Christ's name.*

3. Reliving childhood memories of being cared for and safe helps generate feelings of safety and connection.[6] *Following the Savior's admonition in the Joseph Smith Translation of Mark 14:20–24 and in 3 Nephi 18:7, use the sacrament to remember and contemplate times when Christ has been close to you and you have felt His spirit and love.*

4. Children and teens who know their family history and stories gain a stronger sense of personal identity and are more resilient. Telling, reading, or remembering stories of people being resourceful or resilient seems to prime the brain to try harder after failure, stick with tasks longer, and feel more hopeful about what's possible.[7] *To engage your capacity for spiritual resilience, remember your own difficult times—then also remember how you figured out solutions, found help, got out, survived, stuck with it, or learned. Look for stories of God's protection or of human resourcefulness in scripture,*

history, and especially in your personal or family history. Tell, write, and ponder these stories often, especially when you have a hard task ahead.

5. Help your brain remember loving connections by creating or pondering art or music about the availability and goodness of people.[8] Collect and look at symbols or souvenirs of positive experiences with loved ones. Contemplating these symbols and the stories or attributes associated with them helps people activate their memories of secure attachment and use those memories to feel safer in the present. *You can also collect and reflect on tokens and reminders of spiritual experiences or sacred places to consciously practice settling into your secure attachment with God. Create or ponder artwork and music reminding you of Christ's love and availability, such as pictures of Christ holding a child, embracing an adult, or calming the sea.*

6. Becoming closely involved with a supportive mentor, coach, therapist, or ecclesiastical leader can help people strengthen feelings of connection and heal attachment insecurity, as can joining a supportive group.[9] Group affiliations have the added benefit of giving people opportunities to serve, strengthening their sense of efficacy and worth to others. *Church callings, missions, and temple service also bring people into groups to work, plan, and learn together. You might also discuss with leaders or group members how they conceptualize God, what helps them feel closer to Him, or how they think God feels about you personally and why.*

7. Developing talents or skills helps people feel more capable and able to cope, which can reduce how much energy they have to spend scanning for threats.[10] *Investing in developing your gifts and skills may also help you reduce the time you spend scanning for imagined evidence of God's disapproval or abandonment.*

8. Being in a high-functioning marriage, romantic relationship, close friendship, or extended family increases feelings of attachment security. It also gives people a place to practice the skills of relationship. *Learning the skills of emotional intimacy in long-term committed relationships may be a prerequisite for applying those skills in our relationship with God. Practice being curious, calm, and compassionate with others. Share your honest feelings and fears when appropriate, even when it makes you feel vulnerable. Notice what you expect and desire in a relationship so you understand better what you expect and desire from God. Is what you desire something you know how to receive?*

9. In general, our sense of security in the world and with God is enhanced by anything that increases our sense of:

- Safety—visualize safety now, move out of danger, ask for and receive help, or plan an effective response to problems
- Lovability—receive the gratitude of others; visualize God and others telling you they love you
- Self-soothing and emotional self-regulation—practice relaxation and meditation, exercise, hobbies, walks, positive self-talk, or prayer
- Agency—desire, choose, focus your attention, set goals, and achieve them
- Structure and order—plan, prioritize, and form positive habits
- Relationship repair—apologize, learn from mistakes, and forgive
- Creating meaning—live your values to achieve, help others, live with integrity, and make a difference for good

This is a long (but not exhaustive) list of ways to activate our feelings of security and connection to other people and, indirectly or directly, to God. *Something* on this list can undoubtedly help you feel more grounded in your true status as a beloved daughter or son of God and reinforce your trust in Him.

Learning to Trust the God of Abraham, Step Three: Practice Not Being Anxious about Being Anxious

If you have an anxious attachment style, you may find your anxious feelings getting stirred up often and intensely. Not fun! And because anxiety is not fun, it is easy to get anxious about feeling anxious.

Fear is a normal human experience, a signal that can warn us of danger. But some of us have a broken signal, even with God, like a fire alarm that goes off again and again when there is no fire. If you can't turn off the jumpy alarm, you might ask others for confirmation before you assume you really are in danger of God's (or anyone else's) judgment, abandonment, or overwhelming expectations.

Trying to control anxiety actually makes it worse, however. The more you try to control something you can't control (like feeling anxious) the more out of control (and anxious) you feel. Let me say that again: Trying to control anxiety, which is not controllable, just makes people feel more out of control (and thus more anxious). There is nothing catastrophic about being anxious, even though it is uncomfortable. It is normal, not lethal, and not something you have to completely control or eliminate in order to be a person of faith. That reminder alone can be enough to stop the cycle of anxiety from intensifying.

Learning to Trust the God of Abraham, Step Four: Look for Options You Didn't Have Before

As a child, you may not have had a lot of choices for responding to difficult times. New options you have learned as an adult may be stored someplace in your brain that is not readily accessible to the part of your brain that resonates with old hurts.

Lana faced a potentially lethal illness when her children were still young. Having lost her own father at an early age, Lana was more terrified of subjecting her children to such a devastating and faith-challenging loss than she was of dying. At first Lana couldn't imagine how to protect her kids from pain nobody had protected her from, or how to help them hold onto their trust in the Lord. Friends helped her connect with new possibilities and find comfort in realizing that she could mitigate the impact on her kids in ways no one had mitigated the impact of loss on her. She realized she had time to prepare, include, comfort, and spiritually strengthen her children in ways she had not been prepared, included, comforted, or spiritually strengthened. History did not have to repeat itself. But we don't automatically see such options.

What is an emotionally charged situation that comes up for you now, compromising your trust in the Lord and setting off anxiety instead? Think of one such setting, or notice it when it comes up. Then try these options:

- Name the emotion. Just naming the emotion soothes the brain and initiates coping. (I'm grieving the loss of my innocence. I'm panicking about God's accessibility. I'm angry with God.)
- Look for similarities. When have you experienced similar emotions before? How did you or other people cope? What made it especially hard? How did you experience God then?
- Look for what's different. While there are similarities to your old situation, there are important differences. What options do you have now that you didn't have then? Maybe you can:

a. Explain your point of view to yourself, other people, and the Lord.

b. Take a break, physically or emotionally, by going for a walk, taking some deep breaths, putting on some music, or playing with the dog. Just walking helped people in one study to be substantially more creative,[11] and we need creativity to deal with old threats in new ways. Walking is a great time to pray and ponder.

c. If you are imagining threatening or unkind explanations for another person's behavior, especially God's, think of a possible benevolent explanation, even if it seems far-fetched. Why might God be acting as He is? There is a good chance that the benevolent explanation is more accurate, especially with God.

d. Protect and pray for those you care about. Even if you don't have good role models for how to cope, you don't have to let others suffer in the way you suffered. Ask yourself what you needed that you didn't get. Make things different for those you love by talking to them, offering explanations, listening, making arrangements for their well-being, bringing them closer, writing them letters, praying with them, holding family meetings, sharing your faith, or comforting them in other ways you did not receive.

+ Ask for support. Who could you tell about what you are experiencing? You are not alone now, even if you once were. Others really do love you and want to mourn with you, comfort you, help you, and share your burden (see Mosiah 18:8–9, 27–29). But remember: *they need you to tell them what you're feeling before they can empathize.* And: *they need you to tell them what you need before they can help you get it.* God also expects us to ask, seek, and knock that He might answer us in due time. Humbly exercise faith that He will do so.

+ Change any dysfunctional rules of silence or avoidance you grew up with by instead asking for more information, sharing your feelings, taking charge, letting someone you trust take charge, breaking the problem down into smaller steps, making a joke, or other such strategies. These help you connect with your own resilience, the support of others, and the help of heaven.

+ Remember: an adult is a person who (1) takes responsibility for getting what he or she wants, and (2) takes care of the next generation. How can you step out of your historical childhood role and into your present role of a competent adult who has access to spiritual power?

Learning to Trust the God of Abraham, Step Five: Trust Your Own Resilience

Sometimes bad things happen. Storms rage, wolves howl, unsavory characters threaten, and our gentle walk in the woods turns into a muddy, dangerous mess. When we just want to call a halt to this crazy camping trip and go home, we may assume our only recourse is to plead and cajole and insist until God realizes He needs to *do something* to get things back in control because we can't take anymore.

Except that we probably can take it. We are more resilient than we think. Of course, we don't always want to have to be resilient. We want to be spared. We want things fixed. We want the clock turned back, the heartache undone, the innocence restored. But we are stronger than we know, just as God is more powerful and wise than we know.

God doesn't expect us to be perfect, not at anything, including resilience. But He trusts us to not give up, to choose Him as our Father and God, and to keep going. We don't have to put all our energy into getting God to prevent a future we dread. We can choose to trust ourselves to make it through—with His help.

Learning to Trust the God of Abraham, Step Six: Look for God to Turn Straw into Gold

I believe God's greatest genius is His ability to turn the very worst things into the very best things. The fact that God can turn straw into gold doesn't mean He will take away the straw—the sickness, or heartache, or evil. It does mean He can teach us through the hardest things we experience some of life's most important lessons. It doesn't mean He will eliminate evil from the world. It does mean He can redeem anything He allows to happen and turn it to some good. Sometimes great good. Let's put this to the test. Pause for just one minute to answer three questions:

What has been your biggest failure, loss, or life catastrophe? Write one sentence for it:

_____

What did you learn through that experience that has made you a better person, and that you will never forget? Write down at least one thing:

_____

What do you feel best about in how you handled that trial? Write down at least one thing:

_____

The lessons and personal attributes you learned are the gold God has created from the straw and refuse of *your* life story. These are often the very things that make us more like God—the very things we came to this life to learn.

Job bears his testimony to us about God's power to turn straw into gold, even when we cannot readily perceive His alchemy:

> Behold, I go forward, but he is not there; and backward, but I cannot perceive him:
>
> On the left hand, where he doth work, but I cannot behold him: he hideth himself on the right hand, that I cannot see him:
>
> But he knoweth the way that I take: when he hath tried [honed, developed, purified] me, I shall come forth as gold. (Job 23:8–10)

On the wall of my office is a beautiful painting of my Grandma Mattie when she was in her twenties. Mattie had more than her share of challenges. She sustained a compound fracture of her leg when a teen, and the broken bone visibly protruded from her leg at an odd angle throughout her life. It was literally a miracle that she could walk at all. Rheumatic fever robbed her of much of her hearing. She suffered from painful stomach ulcers. She later broke many more bones in a serious car accident. She didn't marry until she was thirty. Most impactful, she lost her beloved husband after only six years of marriage. She was pregnant with their fourth child at the time. Knowing that he was ill, she had been able to acquire a job before his death, allowing her to provide for her young children. But she worked six days a week; she did not even get the full day off work for her husband's funeral. As a result of hearing her story, exaggerated fears of losing my husband or children have plagued me, especially when our children were young.

Fortunately for me, the stories of my grandmother's courage, humor, spirituality, intelligence, and good cheer also persist through the generations. She served as the first sister missionary for the LDS Church in Oregon and Washington, and my daughters are fourth-generation sister missionaries. She passed on to me the story of seeing my grandfather in a dream after his death, assuring her that he was waiting for her and watching over their family. I knew my grandmother loved and delighted in me. Her trust in God was palpable. Her faith gave me an option of seeing God as loving and available even though the challenges of life are difficult.

I don't like the specter of heartache that seeps through my grandmother's life story to me. Nor did I earn the loving image of God that is also part of her gift and legacy to me. I have had to work hard spiritually to come to trust this God who lets hard things happen to His children, but I have been blessed to leverage my grandmother's gift of faith and make it my own. My secure connection with her and others provides a secure base to my spiritual life. I have seen God turn straw into gold in my grandmother's life. Her story helps me trust that process to be real.

Rachel, referenced earlier, had a different spiritual legacy from mine, and different childhood views of God. Yet as she has willingly followed where light has led her, she has gradually but deliberately chosen to replace those anxiety-provoking images with a different understanding of God. On a recent plane trip, Rachel had the following experience:

> We had to circle the airport for forty-five minutes before we could land this afternoon because high winds had closed the runways. The pilot warned us to be ready for lots of bumps on the way down. That scares me to death. I had just started praying that we could land safely and as easily as possible and I felt God acknowledge to me that He knows my fears.
>
> As I prayed, I thought, "Who am I to pray for this whole plane load of people?" But as I did, I felt God say,

"You are exactly the right person to pray for this plane full of people. And I am going to sit right with you and bring this plane down calmly and safely."

It was pretty amazing. The pilot had had the flight attendants take their seats early, and you could hear the frazzle in his voice. We could feel the plane kind of rock a little bit as we were coming down but, seriously, there was so little in the way of turbulence I think we were all shocked. It felt to me like once the landing gear came down the pilot just steadily powered that plane straight down to the ground. The landing was soft, and you would never have known there was any problem. But once we got on the ground, my seatmate said to me, "I don't think the pilot had any kind of easy time doing that" . . . and the whole plane erupted in applause.

As I write this, I say another prayer of thanks. I believe God honored His word to me and I'm humbled that my prayer of fear—perhaps with many others of other passengers—was heard, responded to, and answered in that way.

All week in my car I've been listening to the hymn "It Is Well with My Soul." I was singing it in my head just before the pilot's announcement.

The lyrics to the hymn that comforted Rachel in the plane were written by Horatio G. Spafford, a devout Christian, in 1873. They not only provided great comfort to a woman whose early images of God terrified her, they provide comfort to me as I try to strengthen the security of my bond with "Our Father which art in heaven," whose kingdom we seek. They are worth savoring as we near the end of this chapter on taming our fears of the future and deepening our trust in God:

When peace, like a river, attendeth my way,
When sorrows like sea billows roll;
Whatever my lot, Thou hast taught me to say,
It is well, it is well with my soul.

Though Satan should buffet, though trials should come,
Let this blest assurance control,
That Christ hath regarded my helpless estate,
And hath shed His own blood for my soul.

My sin—oh, the bliss of this glorious thought!—
My sin, not in part but the whole,
Is nailed to the cross, and I bear it no more,
Praise the Lord, praise the Lord, O my soul! . . .

But, Lord, 'tis for Thee, for Thy coming we wait,
The sky, not the grave, is our goal;
Oh, trump of the angel! Oh, voice of the Lord!
Blessed hope, blessed rest of my soul!

And Lord, haste the day when the faith shall be sight,
The clouds be rolled back as a scroll;
The trump shall resound, and the Lord shall descend,
Even so, it is well with my soul.

Reflecting on her description from ten years ago of a God she saw as only disdainful, indifferent, or dangerous, Rachel concludes:

As I look back, I know those images were there, but, truly, they are gone. I don't see God anymore as a menacing, black, thin, bony, held-back-by-legions-of-angels Being. And I know for certain that I DID see and feel that for so many years. That image is a phantom that arises in my brain when I'm highly anxious or my resources are compromised. But it is an amazement to me, and a gift for which I am profoundly grateful, that my first and persisting image of God today—though sometimes I have to quiet myself to truly see and feel it—is of love.

Children of Israel and Rachel

I change the names of people who have given me permission to use their stories, usually to the first thing that pops into my head. I realized after further pondering her story that my choice of names for "Rachel" may not have been accidental. Rachel, the great matriarch of the house of Israel, had trouble leaving her father's idols behind when she left his house and country. We too can struggle to leave behind the false images of the false gods we have learned of or imagined in our youth. But like both the ancient Rachel and this modern "Rachel," we can choose as adults to discard or ignore the images of God that frighten us and choose instead to invest our faith and trust in the God of light, life, and love. This is a choice we will make many, many times before it becomes natural and automatic. But the more we make that choice, the more peace we find in seeking for God's will to be done.

In *Lectures on Faith*, used by Joseph Smith to teach the Kirtland School of the Prophets for early Church leaders, we learn that in order to "exercise faith in God unto life and salvation" we must have "a *correct* idea of his character, perfections, and attributes" (italics in the original). These attributes include that He is "merciful and gracious, slow to anger, abundant in goodness, and that he was so from everlasting to everlasting . . . that he is a God of truth and cannot lie . . . [and] that he is love."[12]

Ultimately, this is the only God there is. We can afford to trust Him completely when we pray for His will to be done, His kingdom to come. No matter what has happened or will happen, He has the *will* and the *power* to save us, and He is always on our side.

(Note: See the Appendix for additional questions and exercises.)

Chapter 7

PRACTICING STILLNESS
IN THE PRESENT

—⟨⊷✦⊶⟩—

Yea, he saith: Come unto me and ye shall partake
of the fruit of the tree of life; yea, ye shall eat and
drink of the bread and the waters of life freely.

(ALMA 5:34)

I love bread: white bread, brown bread, potato bread, and sour-dough bread; zucchini bread, pumpkin bread, raisin bread, and banana bread; bagels, baguettes, bread sticks, tortillas, flat bread, pita bread, and naan. I love the smell of bread, the look of bread. I even love bread dough. I especially love bread fresh out of the oven. Given half a chance, I will eat bread like there's no tomorrow.

This is not a good idea, however. I may love bread, but when I eat bread like there's no tomorrow, bread doesn't love me. It sits in my stomach like a rock. All is not well in Zion. When I try to eat enough bread today to last me through a week from Tuesday, I remember the hard way what the Lord tried to teach the Israelites with manna, "the bread which the Lord hath given" (Exodus 16:15). The Lord fed them this bread every morning, day in and day out, for forty years. If they overslept or got distracted, they didn't eat, for manna melted with the rising sun. But if they doubted the reliability of the supply chain or thought they could cash in if they saved some for tomorrow, it got worms and stank. No matter how much or how little a person gathered each day, when they measured it "he that gathered much had nothing over, and he that gathered little had no lack" (v. 18). Gorging was senseless and hoarding useless in a world God littered daily with bread. This must have been very hard for the control freaks in the crowd.

The Lord's Prayer for daily bread hearkens back to this amazing miracle in the history of Israel. For decades, as the Jehovah of the Old Testament, Jesus Christ had provided that bread. Now, in the New Testament, the Provider becomes the Supplicant. When He prays, "Give us this day our daily bread," He both joins us in our hunger and tutors us in trust that God will provide day by day what we truly need.

We've discussed in previous chapters how our history can intrude on our relationship with God when we expect Him to be no better than the humans who have disappointed or neglected us. We've also discussed how fear of the future can lead us to both lose touch with our resilience and stop daring to hope for miracles. But with our prayer for bread today, we remember that the past exists only in our memory, the future only in our imagination, and that we can live only in the present, the eternal now. Right now, for today, we have enough. Our task is to see, gather, and partake of God's *ever-present* miracles today.

Gather, Bake, and Eat with God

We are not languishing in the wilderness, and God expects us today to plant and harvest, plan and store up so that we will have the bread we need in the months ahead. Nevertheless, I need to gather God to me every day or I will go hungry indeed. Miraculously, as I receive God today, I get double blessings: out of His store, I can both eat what He provides and lay it up as treasure in heaven.

Talking with God each day is a wonderful privilege. As we express our concerns, share our feelings, and articulate our goals and needs, we build a relationship in which we can feel known and supported. But prayer is not the only way I gather God to me each day. The world is His table, His studio, His home, and His temple, and our work, creativity, relationships, and worship are also forms of prayer that support our relationship with Him.

Full-time missionaries generally learn early that *everything* they do (exercising, studying, planning, grooming, eating, inviting, teaching, and resting) is not only consecrated to the Lord but essential to their ability to receive the Spirit and succeed in their work. After their missions, they often wonder how they can have the Spirit to be with them when their lives are now, necessarily, focused on school, work, and social engagements that are more about "selfish" pursuits than dedicated service to others. It takes some doing to realize that God is willing and eager to be with them in *all* things, not just *His* things. Just as He wants those returning missionaries to continue to engage in His work, He wants to join them in theirs. Our work is also His work.

Even though I believe God is willing to come along for every kind of ride I take, it takes some effort and self-awareness on my part to remember God *always*, not just when I'm on my knees or immersed in the scriptures. It can be especially hard to remember Him when work feels overwhelming, challenges bog me down, or relationship problems consume me. But frankly, when things are humming along nicely, God can also be far from the thoughts and intents of my heart. Apparently, there is no shortage of reasons to forget or overlook the evidence of God's love.

Nor is there a shortage of reasons to remember it. Elizabeth Barrett Browning wrote:

> *Earth's crammed with heaven,*
> *And every common bush afire with God;*
> *But only he who sees, takes off his shoes.*[1]

If I tune my eyes to see, even the most "common bushes" of my life—the work activities, creative projects, and recreational delights of any given day—can build my relationships, including with God. Especially with God. Our engagement with each present moment can nourish our relationship with our Father, our Savior, and our Comforter.

One Bite at a Time

There are so many hungers we can fill only one moment at a time—hungers for connection, meaning, purpose, beauty, learning, and love. For example, each day I need to gather spiritual sustenance. Some days I gather little and some days much. If I don't gather, I won't eat, and I'll get spiritually cranky. If I stuff myself today, I'll still need to eat tomorrow. And even if I can't gather all I think I need, God can make it—and me—enough.

Sometimes, though, the nourishment I need comes in the form of challenges that feel too big to swallow. I learned from my daughter Carrie the importance of breaking such bread into bite-sized pieces before stuffing it into my mouth. Otherwise, I can choke on the very things God is sending to nourish and bless me. Let me explain.

Carrie's mission had been organized for only three years when she arrived in it. The local economy was underdeveloped, and most people were poor and unhappy. Americans were unwelcome and Mormons misunderstood. Her mission president made a big pile in his backyard of the rocks people threw at his house. Her first branch president, though a college graduate, conducted church in pajama bottoms, as those were his only pants. Carrie struggled with the language, the living conditions, and the responsibility she felt to help people find the nourishment of the gospel. Every day was hard. She often felt like she was trying to make five loaves and two small fishes feed not only herself but entire cities for months at a time. In other words, she was a missionary!

When she felt overwhelmed with all her responsibilities and all the needs around her, Carrie learned to say again and again, "All I have to do right now is _____." All I have to do right now is find the bus stop. All I have to do right now is knock on this door. All I have to do right now is teach this lesson, study the language, fix dinner, make a plan, go to sleep. Taken individually, each of these things was manageable, and if it wasn't manageable she could break it down to something simpler: All I have to do now is get out the map, peel this carrot, put on my coat, say hello.

As long as she didn't allow herself to face all the needs and hungers of an entire mission at once, she had enough each moment to meet that moment's need. She had enough of today's bread for today, and she learned to trust there would be enough of tomorrow's bread tomorrow. Or in an hour.

Nephi is a great example of this principle. While Laman and Lemuel long for the security they remembered in the past or scoff at the impossibility of success in the future, Nephi takes on one challenge at a time, one piece at a time. He doesn't need to see how it will all work out before he steps into the dark. His bow breaks and they are all threatened with starvation? All he has to do right now is find wood for a new one. God wants him to build a ship that will traverse the ocean? All he has to do right now is find ore for tools. He needs to get the brass plates from Laban? All he has to do right now is go back into the city and wait upon the Lord. He writes, "And I was led by the Spirit, not knowing beforehand the things which I should do" (1 Nephi 4:6).

I've passed Carrie's simple mantra on to thousands of people, but sometimes it is still hard for me to remember. When I do remember, then "All I have to do right now is fix this paragraph" can be enough to keep me writing, and eventually the book gets finished. "All I have to do right now is talk to my husband" invites the empathy I long for even when my loneliness feels bottomless. "All I have to do right now is get out the oatmeal, email for an appointment, put on my shoes, read a few verses" gets breakfast ready, visits made, exercise done, spirit nourished—one mouthful at a time. I am freed from the intensity of demand to notice the spiritual resources available right now, in this moment, to bless me. My heart is free to rejoice in the carrot, the map, the paragraph, the "common bushes" that are afire with God.

Dwelling on the past, I can feel captured and held hostage by things I cannot change. Projecting myself into the future, I can float untethered amid countless threats and risks. But in this present moment, all that is left of the past is what God has redeemed, and all that the future holds is the fulfillment of God's promises. In this single dot that stands between the past and the future, I can choose to be a ghost, a mirage . . . or joyfully, deeply alive.

1. *Work with God in the present: All I have to do right now is* _____ (fill in the blank).

Grateful in *All* Things

I have always loved this story, told by John Lyman Smith:

In my early years I used to eat often at the table with Joseph the Prophet. At one time he was called to dinner. I was at play in the room with his son Joseph when he called us to him, and we stood one on each side of him. After he had looked over the table he said, "Lord, we thank Thee for this johnny cake, and ask Thee to send us something better.

Amen." The cornbread was cut and I received a piece from his hand.

Before the bread was all eaten, a man came to the door and asked if the Prophet Joseph was at home.

Joseph replied he was, whereupon the visitor said, "I have brought you some flour and a ham."

Joseph arose and took the gift, and blessed the man in the name of the Lord. Turning to his wife, Emma, he said, "I knew the Lord would answer my prayer."[2]

It was obviously quite memorable for a young boy to see the prophet's prayer for "something better" answered so dramatically, albeit simply. I've also never forgotten that what opened the door to that "something better" was Joseph Smith's prayer of gratitude for a dinner consisting only of cornbread.

Generating feelings of gratitude is not only good for the soul, it is good for the heart and the brain, easing both into benevolent rhythms that nurture creativity and calm. While it is annoyingly impossible to just "choose" to be happy, we *can* choose to be grateful, and other good feelings often follow. When I got tired a few years ago of repeating the same list of requests night and morning in prayer, I decided to prepare for sleep by telling the Lord about my day instead—not making any requests, but praying only gratitude. It is delightful to review the day with my Father in Heaven from this perspective. I tell Him my favorite parts of the day. I bless the names of those who have loved and helped me. I look for lessons in difficult experiences or challenges. I relive and savor what I'm grateful for and notice what I, or others, had to do to make those things happen, expanding my gratitude. One of those "others" is unfailingly God.

My friend Dana Israelson[3] has taught me again and again the merit of the scripture, "Thou shalt thank the Lord thy God in all things" (Doctrine and Covenants 59:7). Dana speaks of reminding herself often that this scripture does not say to be grateful for good things or favorable circumstances, but "all things." She has learned that when she is genuinely, continuously grateful, she learns how all things, even hard things, can bring miracles, blessings, learning, and growth.

Dana has gotten plenty of practice over the years I've known her. Recently Dana learned something about manna when a business associate of her husband, Brent, called to say Brent was acting strangely and they were heading for the hospital. Brent is diabetic, so Dana thought his blood sugar was just low, but when she arrived at the hospital she learned that Brent had had a massive stroke. Five doctors and several nurses were working to save his life. One stepped out just long enough to tell Dana he had no time to be subtle: if she had children in the area, she should call them to come immediately, as he didn't expect Brent to live.

Brent did live, and he is making an unexpected and remarkable recovery, but Dana spent long, poignant hours in the hospital at his bedside and many months helping him at home. Then, the day after Brent got his driver's license back, Dana learned that she had lung cancer that had spread throughout her body. She began her own precarious road of treatments, recovery, and miracles. Their financial situation is still precarious and their future opaque. But Dana testifies:

> God provides the manna we need to sustain us, one day at a time. If I start to worry about the future, I become completely overwhelmed and paralyzed. But when I am grateful in *all things*, even hard things, there are miracles all around me. Gratitude for my trials moves me to a place of humility where I can feel my Savior's love, access His Spirit, and receive strength beyond my own. It opens up

a space for me to trust that He will consecrate this trial to my good. I can be cheerful and calm. There is enough, and to spare.

Smell the aroma of miracles baking. Gather blessings that distill with the morning dew, just enough for today.

1. *Work with God in the present: All I have to do right now is* _____.

2. *Thank God in the present: Whatever is going on, right now I am grateful that* _____ (fill in this blank).

Willingly Hungry

Of course, when my stomach is growling, I can get *really* impatient for the timer to go off signaling the miracles are ready and the manna distilled. But being hungry also has its place. The Savior teaches, "Blessed are all they who do hunger and thirst after righteousness, for they shall be filled with the Holy Ghost" (3 Nephi 12:6).

When Candace's marriage started to founder, she was starving for answers. Wanting to do all she could to merit them, she fasted for twenty-four hours every Friday, went to the temple each week, completely avoided secular music and TV, read the lessons for Sunday School, studied the scriptures nightly, and faithfully served in her calling. "What more can I do to get help with this marriage?" she pled. The impression came, "Do your visiting teaching." She wondered what visiting teaching could possibly have to do with her marital challenges. Nevertheless, she did her visiting teaching. Hungry for help, she was open to following even this quiet spiritual "hunch" she might otherwise have ignored. Doing so tutored her in the language of the Spirit and strengthened her confidence in the principle of revelation.

Says Joseph Smith:

> When you feel pure intelligence flowing into you, it may give you sudden strokes of ideas, so that by noticing it, you may find it fulfilled the same day or soon; (i.e.) those things that were presented unto your minds by the Spirit of God, will come to pass; and thus by learning the Spirit of God and understanding it, you may grow into the principle of revelation, until you become perfect in Christ Jesus.[4]

Sometimes we assume other people are privy to a gift of revelation God for some reason doesn't bestow on us. But Joseph Smith seems to imply here that we can "grow into the principle of revelation" by "noticing" sudden bits of ideas, seeing what "comes to pass" as we act on them, and learning by experience.

Visiting teaching had always been hard for Candace, so doing it when she was already so stressed felt doubly difficult. But visiting teaching helped Candace make a friend. That friend needed support, but she also provided it to Candace. That friend's sister later bought Candace's house when she needed to move, and the house just happened to be right next to the sister's son's school. Candace gained spiritual confidence, and her friend gained tender mercies for her family. All because Candace was hungry enough to follow even the slightest, quietest hunch about what the Spirit might be telling her to do.

Candace didn't give her last bread away to someone who dined while she starved. All got helped. All got fed. God doesn't take advantage of one person just to help someone else He cares about more. In fact, I know God's economy is in play when I can't tell if I'm giving or receiving. When we put our hunger on the altar, He uses it to feed the world. In turn He consecrates His spiritual wealth to our blessing and hands over to us His love.

Candace later wrote, "At the time it felt like all I got was silence for days and weeks at a time. But looking back, I realize God gave me answers as fast as I could make any use of them, as fast as I could tolerate them. I also realize He was always with me in it. It was just hard to see at the time."

It *is* hard to see it at the time. It was even hard for the Israelites to see manna at the time. *Manna* means, "What is it?" They probably called it manna because they had no clue what it was or what to do with it. I would probably have put it more strongly: "What in the world is that supposed to be? We're supposed to eat *that?* When is the *real* food coming? This stuff can't possibly fill us up. When am I going to get some answers I know what to do with? *Do my visiting teaching?* What kind of an answer is that? I need answers with some meat in them." But when I act on quiet impressions and see spiritual results, I am fed with what I need most: assurance that God is with me.

Our bishop told the ward at a recent testimony meeting:

> I give to charities to help the poor, but as a matter of principle I don't give to people begging on the street. In fact, beggars are sort of a pet peeve of mine. However, I recently made a commitment to act on anything that might be a spiritual prompting, rather than to rationalize or dismiss it as only my own silly idea. Last week, after driving by a man in a wheelchair who was begging, I thought I heard, "Go help that man." So I went back, and I helped. As I drove away, the man called out, "God bless you, sir!" In that simple moment, I felt like I *was* being blessed, and I was deeply moved. I felt how much God wants to bind up all of our wounds. We can know how much God loves us by following the whispering of the Spirit to help someone

else. When I felt God's love for that man in the wheelchair, I felt His love for me.

When I am hungry for answers, it can be tempting to treat God like an indifferent waiter who is slow with the food I'm craving, or to turn away in disgust when what shows up at the table looks unfamiliar or insufficient. But when I am hungry not just for answers but for God and for righteousness, even a stranger on a visiting teaching roster or a beggar in a wheelchair can be a harbinger of God's love for me. I'm more willing to "try just one bite" of things I don't normally eat, and I learn to *"taste and see* that the Lord is good: [and that] *blessed* is the man that trusteth in him" (Psalm 34:8).

How grateful I am for the spiritual hunger that helps me say, with the Psalmist:

> As the deer pants for streams of water, so my soul pants for you, O God.
> My soul thirsts for God, for the living God. When can I go and meet with God?
> (Psalm 42:1–2, New International Version; I appreciate the NIV's emphasis on meeting with God rather than appearing before Him.)

Perhaps it is only deep hunger and thirst for the Spirit that teaches us to say, with Job, "I have esteemed the words of his mouth *more than my necessary food"* (Job 23:12), or, in keeping with the theme of this chapter, *"more than my daily bread"* (Job 23:12, New International Version). When we are hungry enough, we willingly act on anything that has the slightest whiff of a spiritual prompting, because following the aroma of Living Bread will lead us to what we are most hungry for.

1. *Work with God in the present: All I have to do right now is
   _____.*
2. *Thank God in the present: Whatever is going on, right now I
   am grateful that _____.*
3. *Taste and see in the present: Even though I'm unsure, I will act
   on this quiet hunch to _____* (fill in this blank).

God, Our Necessary Food

When our early deficits and traumas have trained our brain to
distrust, even hearty eaters can become spiritually anorexic, holding God's nourishing presence at arm's length lest we become too
dependent on something we cannot control. Like Israelites in slavery, when we've been tutored in assumptions of scarcity and threat
from a young age, we have a hard time laying them aside. Some of
us anxiously cling to people we assume are grown-up enough to
keep us safe and fed; then we feel perplexed and betrayed when
they fail us. Other times we insist we can handle life alone, and
we become indifferent or disdainful toward others, then find ourselves starving, lonely, and wondering why. Sometimes we have to
patiently train ourselves to have an appetite for God.

When Linda was raising two toddlers, working part-time,
serving in the Primary, and building a house, life got a little crazy.
Perhaps because she had so much to do, she found herself assuming God had a lot to do also, and that He was undoubtedly too
busy for her. But she wasn't that eager to talk with Him anyway.
She felt ashamed that she wasn't attending the temple, holding
family home evening, doing her visiting teaching, or even praying
with any consistency, and that she didn't even want to.

With the start of a new year, Linda decided something needed
to change in her relationship with God. She also knew any change
would have to be really small and unarguably easy or she just

wouldn't do it. Finally, she made a goal to sit still for fifteen minutes twice a week, and to ask God to sit with her. Sitting still for fifteen minutes didn't seem like it should be all that hard, and inviting God to sit with her seemed unthreatening enough. After all, it wasn't like God was going to come and sit on the couch with her, so she didn't need to worry about what uncomfortable feelings might come up if He *really* came.

When Linda first tried replacing *The List* with *The Sit*, it turned out to be a whole lot harder than she had anticipated. At first, she resisted her sitting time because she was sure nothing would happen anyway and it felt like a waste of precious time she could be using to do something worthwhile. But as she stuck with her plan, she realized a deeper fear undergirded her resistance. She was deeply afraid that, if given the chance, God would just add a big bunch of stuff to *The List* and then walk away, going back to His very important life and leaving her to manage alone.

To Linda's surprise, as she made it a priority to simply sit, it really did feel like God came and sat with her. What's more, He was a gentleman and played by her rules. He didn't speak unless invited, and He didn't push any agenda. When she sat, He sat. She decided to bring a paper and pen to *The Sit* and to write down anything that came up. What came up early was *The List*: all the things she knew she should be doing and wasn't. She just wrote it all down and looked it over. It felt long and overwhelming, as always. She said in her heart to the One sitting beside her, "Okay, Heavenly Father, where do you want me to begin? I can't do all of this, and I certainly can't do it all at once, but I can do something. Where should I start?" She felt the answer, slow and gentle, "These are all good things. You can do whatever you like. But this is not what I care about right now. I care about you."

That one makes me cry.

Only after several weeks did she "hear" the words, "There *is* something I'd like you to work on: Enjoy your children."

Ah, yes. This is the God I know.

When Linda made the time to sit patiently through her resistance, fear, and sorrow and invited God to sit with her, He came. And He came with only love, not a list, in His hand. To her surprise, as Linda let in God's loving acceptance, she found herself tackling some of the items on *The List* with more patience and hope. She still finds it hard to take the time to sit still, or to tolerate the closeness she both longs for and fears with a God she still doesn't completely trust to be on her side. But God still comes and sits, often, and He still waits patiently for her when she waits for Him.

The thought of sitting patiently brings to mind, of all things, my eating habits. When it comes to food, I'm sort of a grazer. As a result, I don't always take the time to sit and be truly present with what I'm eating. I tend to scarf food down without really enjoying it, as if it might get away from me if I held it more lightly. I noticed recently that I say "grazing" prayers, too. Even when I talk to God a lot, I don't necessarily take time to sit still with God, to take Him in, to really be present. So I love the image of Linda, sitting in a "love seat" with God, just inviting Him close. No agenda. Writing down what comes up. Savoring these minutes that He is with her.

Linda concludes:

> I find it so interesting that after Christ dies, His Apostles just go back to work. They go off to their boats and start fishing. What's that about? It's like they suddenly get all nervous about not having enough to eat, or enough to do. But it isn't Christ telling them to get busy. While they're off fishing, Christ is just sitting there on the lake shore making breakfast and wanting to talk about love. When He tells them where to cast their nets for more fish,

He reminds them that He is God over all these ways we try to feed ourselves. But He also shows them that what's really important to Him is them.

I have always loved this image of the risen Savior, unobtrusively cleaning fish, kneading bread, tending a fire to coals, cooking food, and inviting His Apostles to eat. Savor these words and this meal for a moment:

> As soon then as [the Apostles] were come to land, they saw a fire of coals there, and fish laid thereon, and bread.
>
> Jesus saith unto them, Bring of the fish which ye have now caught.
>
> Simon Peter went up, and drew the net to land full of great fishes, an hundred and fifty and three: and for all there were so many, yet was not the net broken.
>
> Jesus saith unto them, Come and dine. . . .
>
> Jesus then cometh, and taketh bread, and giveth them, and fish likewise. . . .
>
> So when they had dined, Jesus saith to Simon Peter, Simon, son of Jonas, lovest thou me more than these? He saith unto him, Yea, Lord; thou knowest that I love thee. He saith unto him, Feed my lambs. . . .
>
> Feed my sheep. (John 21:9–17)

At first the Apostles don't notice the stranger on the shore. He's just sitting there, cooking in the sand. They don't really notice Him on the road to Emmaus, either. He's just walking there, moving along in the dirt. It has taken me a long time to realize that I don't notice Him either, sitting on the love seat, waiting for me to finish my very important work and sit too.

Peter later writes to the Church, in words reminiscent of this poignant experience and conversation with the Savior:

Feed the flock of God which is among you, taking the oversight thereof, not by constraint, but willingly; not for filthy lucre, but of a ready mind;

Neither as being lords over God's heritage, but being ensamples to the flock. . . .

Casting all your care upon him; for he careth for you. (1 Peter 5:2–3, 7)

Each of us has a work to do: a house to build, a table to fill, a new generation to care for. There isn't anything wrong with fishing. Sometimes we can learn as much about God in a fishing boat as in any other place. There isn't anything wrong with driving a pizza truck or balancing a spreadsheet, with studying for chemistry class or doing the laundry—unless our "very important work" keeps us from recognizing the Stranger on the shore. Staying connected with God gives our work, our recreation, our relationships, and all our daily rituals new meaning.

God's very important work is us. Caring for us, and teaching us to care for each other, *is His work*. We have the privilege of being engaged in the work of God, and a primary way we build our relationship with Him is to feed His sheep. Even when we, like His ancient disciples, forget exactly what our mission is and what we know of Christ, He willingly joins us in our work, telling us where to cast our nets and cooking breakfast for us while we do. But whether we are working for Him or He is working for us, sometimes we simply need to put down our nets, throw ourselves into the water, and swim with all our might toward the cookfire of Christ. When we cast all our care upon Him in complete trust that He will feed and care for us, any work becomes a mission, and any role we take becomes discipleship. Working side by side with the Lord builds our relationship with Him.

But work can still tire and stress us. It isn't a sin to be tired, tense, tempted, or hungry, although Satan is eager to use our mortal weakness to drag us into sin and convince us there is not enough. The Lord, in contrast, is eager to love us, feed us, and hold us. Sometimes we have to come to His table to be fed; often we also have to notice that He is knocking. We then have to open *our* door and invite Him to join *our* table: "Behold, I stand at the door, and knock: if any man hear my voice, and open the door, I will come in to him, and will sup with him, and he with me" (Revelation 3:20).

1. *Work with God in the present: All I have to do right now is* _____.
2. *Thank God in the present: Whatever is going on, right now I am grateful that* _____.
3. *Taste and see in the present: Even though I'm unsure, I will act on this quiet hunch to* _____.
4. *Be still in the present: Invite God close, and write down what comes up.*

Remember

Even after forty days of fasting, Christ tells the tempter and reminds us, "Man shall not live by bread alone, but by every word that proceedeth out of the mouth of God" (Matthew 4:4). He later adds to His Apostles, "I have meat to eat that ye know not of. . . . My meat is to do the will of him that sent me, and to finish his work" (John 4:32–34). The food we need most is made not of wheat or corn but of love and presence.

In sacrament meeting one week, I connected with the prayer from the sacrament table that God would "bless and sanctify this bread to the souls of all those who partake of it, *that they may eat in remembrance* of the body of thy Son, and witness unto thee, O God, the Eternal Father, that they are willing to take upon them the name of thy Son, and always remember him" (Doctrine and Covenants 20:77).

The Savior instituted the sacrament at His last meal with His Apostles. The Joseph Smith Translation of Mark 14:20–21 adds the important words in italics below, indicating more specifically what we are to remember about Him:

> And as they did eat, Jesus took bread and blessed it, and brake, and gave to them, and said, Take it, and eat.
>
> *Behold, this is for you to do in remembrance of my body; for as oft as ye do this ye will remember this hour that I was with you.*

The sacrament prayer doesn't specifically state that we "eat *this bread* in remembrance," but that we "*eat* in remembrance." In other words, every time we put food into our mouths can be an opportunity to remember the condescension of Christ. He joins us in the mortal condition of hunger and thirst, and He provides the daily bread to nourish us body and soul and to make us enough for whatever He asks us to experience or do.

But the verses above also remind me that I am not just trying to remember His suffering and death. I am to eat in remembrance of *each hour that He has been with me*, gratefully savoring again the ways He has fed me. When He knows His time on earth is marching toward its inevitable and unimaginably difficult climax, He doesn't focus His disciples' attention on all that is about to go wrong. Instead, He invites them to remember the life He is at that very moment sharing so intimately with them, and to remember what they have seen, heard, learned, and felt in His presence at His table.

Each week, He invites me, too, to this remembrance. Even heavenly manna may feed me only for today, but remembering the hours Christ has been with me can continue to feed me for a lifetime. When I slow down to the speed of life, gratefully savoring today's bread today, I begin to recognize that in this very moment, the whole world is the table of the Lord. I sit, always, at His table, His bounty lovingly spread before me, if I have eyes to see.

Chapter 8

OBTAINING
DELIVERANCE FROM EVIL

Forgive us our debts, as we forgive our debtors.
And lead us not into temptation, but deliver us from evil.
(MATTHEW 6:12–13)

Following the outline of the Lord's Prayer, we've looked at the impact on our relationship with God of three things: assumptions we acquire from our past, expectations we hold for the future, and our capacity for conscious presence in the here and now. The Lord's Prayer reminds us next that a dark thread weaves through all these time periods. In opposition to the light and love of God we seek are the pervasive realities of evil, temptation, and sin.

Exposure to the evil in the world can leave us doubting the power, wisdom, or benevolence of God. Likewise, experience with "the temptations and the sins which do so easily beset" us (1 Nephi 4:18) can leave us doubting ourselves and our capacity to ever merit or relate to our perfect Father. How can we obtain deliverance from the evil in the world and in us so that we can feel at home in the kingdom, power, and glory of God upon which the Lord's Prayer concludes? How can we be delivered from evil so we can taste, trust, and receive the love of God?

Our experience with evil varies, but none of us is immune.

One of the most distressing phone calls I ever received came late one evening while my husband, Dave, fairly recently sustained as the bishop of our ward, was out of town on business. The caller identified himself as a representative of the Federal Aviation Administration (FAA). My heart raced as I scrambled to remember if Dave was supposed to be on a plane that night. The call was not about Dave, however, but about Bob, his counselor in the bishopric. Bob, who worked for the FAA and who was also away on business at the time, had been found murdered in his hotel room. The FAA representative was at the home of his widow, who wanted us to come. I will never forget the wrenching experience of telling one of Bob's daughters as she returned home from babysitting that night that someone had killed her father, or waking Bob's mother who lived with them to inform her of her son's senseless death.

Bob was truly one of the happiest, warmest people I have ever met. He had a friendly sense of humor, a solid faith, and a down-to-earth personality. I couldn't imagine him deliberately hurting anyone, nor could I imagine why anyone would hurt him. His killers took $40 and some credit cards. His murder has not been solved.

By any definition, the crime that widowed a good woman and left five children without their father was an evil act. Fifteen years later, Bob's wife and children, surrounded by the love and support of friends, family, and ward members and sustained by the Spirit, have found a remarkable degree of healing, hope, and even happiness. They are, like their husband and father, cheerful, warm, friendly people with down-to-earth personalities and great faith. Their paths have not been easy. But somehow, God has delivered them from the grasp of this evil, making it possible for them to grow up, love others, and trust Him in spite of it.

Assuring our opportunity for deliverance from evil, whether

outside us or inside us, is a major purpose of the Atonement of Christ. As Jesus concluded the Last Supper and prepared for Gethsemane and Golgotha, He left His blessing on His disciples whom He sent out into the world:

> I pray not that thou shouldest take them out of the world, but that thou shouldest keep them from the evil. . . . Neither pray I for these alone, but for them also which shall believe on me through their word; That they all may be one; as thou, Father, art in me, and I in thee, that they also may be one in us . . . that they may be made perfect in one. (John 17:15, 20–21, 23)

As we are among those who believe through the words of Christ's Apostles, He prayed for each of us that night in Jerusalem. If your life has been tainted by serious evil, Christ's prayers specifically include you. His pleas that we will find *deliverance* from evil (both in the passage above and in the Lord's Prayer) do not spare us from *contact* with evil, however. Evil is ever before us all, working its insidious and divisive effects on our relationships with other people and with God.

We could rightly define evil as that which estranges us from ourselves, from other people, and from God. Both the evil we experience and the evil we commit thwart our willingness and ability to love. But as we follow Christ's teachings and example, we can overcome the estranging impact of evil on our relationships.

Evil in the World

Fortunately, relatively few of us are the victims of such senseless and devastating violence as were Bob and his family. Not so fortunately, all of us are affected, directly or indirectly, by evil. As just one example, in a large study of 17,421 mostly white, middle-class, middle-aged, well-educated, and financially secure individuals completing an extensive medical screening questionnaire, only a third had not been affected as children by either divorce, abuse (physical, emotional, or sexual), significant parental neglect, or parents who were mentally ill, addicted, or imprisoned. One in ten reported having been *frequently* sworn at, insulted, or put down by parents or caretakers. More than one in four said a parent had *repeatedly* pushed them, slapped them, thrown things at them, or hit them hard enough to leave a mark or injury. Sexual abuse was reported by 28 percent of women and 16 percent of men. One in eight had seen their mother *frequently* pushed, hit, kicked, bitten, or slapped. Almost 90 percent of those who had experienced one of these categories had experienced more than one, magnifying their impact.[1] While I don't know how representative this data is of Church members in general, these unexpectedly high numbers are apparently the sobering realities for many in the world we live in.

One researcher compared the health of people who had this type of history with the health of people without such direct contact with family disruption or violence. He concluded that the most serious and costly public health issue in the United States today is child abuse. The national price tag for the medical costs, both immediate and long-term, of people abused, neglected, or exposed to violence as children exceeds the costs of cancer or heart disease. These children grow into adults who are more than twice as likely to be depressed, three times as likely to be alcoholic, and four times as likely to commit suicide, use IV drugs, or participate in domestic violence themselves, continuing its devastating cycle in the next generation.[2] Perhaps we are not so far from the days of Noah, to whom the Lord said, "The end of all flesh is come before me, for the earth is filled with violence" (Moses 8:30).

Although living in poverty certainly does not make a person

evil, the existence of poverty in the world is a poignant reminder that we who are not poor have a ways to go if we want to "walk guiltless before God" (Mosiah 4:26). Today, 51 percent of America's schoolchildren qualify for free or reduced-price lunch at school because of the level of poverty in their homes.[3] Poverty is a major contributing factor to poor attachment because of the disruption it creates in children's lives,[4] and poor attachment correlates with a wide variety of mental illnesses and other long-term problems. Kids in poverty are far less likely to even consider college, have any idea how to get into college, be prepared to succeed at college, or graduate from college.[5]

My purpose in recounting the story of Bob and summarizing the above research is not to shout that the sky is falling, however. We live in a mortal existence in which God permits evil that we might learn by our own experience how we feel about it and what we will do about it. God stands ready to teach us how to use our experience here to mature our spirits, deepen our faith, and cherish one another more. But Satan is also at the ready, eager to prove God wrong about the benefits and possibilities inherent in both agency and love.

Two Kingdoms

Evil is synonymous with profound wickedness, immorality, malevolence, and depravity. From a gospel perspective, evil results from actions that oppose or seek to undermine the sovereignty of God. Love permeates and flows from God's kingdom, and God's righteous reign is characterized by the integrity, humility, agency, peace, order, commitment, and fairness that make loving connections flourish. The same characteristics that strengthen our companionship with one another allow us to have the constant companionship of the Holy Ghost and rightfully participate in the governance of

God's Church and kingdom on earth (see Doctrine and Covenants 121:36–46).

By contrast, Satan attempts to gain the upper hand in the world through deception, hubris, force, violence, chaos, hatred, indifference, self-indulgence, and injustice. His work creates enmity on every side, driving wedges between people and alienating them from God. His governing principles also alienate us from ourselves as we participate in self-deception and self-destruction. To sin is to believe Satan over God about what will make us happy or the world better. To sin is to ignore the painful consequences of our behavior on us and other people. When we reject the slow, careful process of drawing others to us by selfless love, or allowing ourselves to be drawn to God by His perfect and humble affections, and instead force our will on others, we act in direct opposition to God's loving and righteous rule.

Being a victim of others' evil is traumatizing, and children are even more deeply affected than adults by exposure to traumatic loss, violence, or betrayal. As scary as earthquakes and car crashes are, being the victim of a random natural event or accident is not nearly as traumatizing as being deliberately sinned against by another human being. When that human being is someone we have trusted, loved, and depended on, the negative impact compounds. Terror, rage, despair, paralysis, numbness, shame, and grief are only some of the possible consequences. Traumatic betrayal damages and sickens our brains, our health, and our relationships.

The evil from which we need deliverance is not limited to the dramatic or violent sins of others. In addition, awareness of our own sins and capacity for evil can sicken and distress us, disrupting our relationships with other people and with God. When Tom inadvertently led his squadron into an ambush during the Vietnam War, every member of his platoon was killed or wounded within seconds by hidden gunmen. Tom watched helplessly as his best friend died. Flashbacks and nightmares followed. Even years later, sounds or images reminiscent of the ambush brought back all the terror and rage he had experienced that day. But the hardest part of the whole experience was not what was done to Tom, but what Tom subsequently did. The day after the attack, Tom responded to the deaths of his friends with a frenzy of unspeakable violence upon the men, women, and children of a neighboring village. His therapist reports:

> After that it became truly impossible for him to go home again in any meaningful way. How can you face your sweetheart . . . or watch your son take his first step when you are reminded of the [horrible violence you committed against women and children]? Tom experienced the death of [his friend] as if part of himself had been forever destroyed—the part that was good and honorable and trustworthy. Trauma, whether it is the result of something done to you or something you yourself have done, almost always makes it difficult to engage in intimate relationships. After you have experienced something so unspeakable, how do you learn to trust yourself or anyone else again? Or, conversely, how can you surrender to an intimate relationship after you have been brutally violated?[6]

The Lord's Prayer is not only a plea to be spared or released from evil influences "out there," threatening us with violence and deception. We also need deliverance from evil that seems to get inside us. Unless we are very, very careful, the evil we fight and seek to destroy can insidiously shape us in its image. Our own capacity for evil can be activated when we become preoccupied with the evil in others. Thus Christ teaches, "resist not evil. . . . Love your enemies, bless them that curse you, do good to them that hate you, and pray for them which despitefully use you, and persecute you" (Matthew 5:39, 44). We don't overcome Satan by facing him down for a fight but by turning our backs to him and our faces toward God and His righteousness. The Savior said to Satan, "Get thee behind me, Satan: for it is written, Thou shalt worship the Lord thy God and him only shalt thou serve" (Luke 4:8).

	Outside Ourselves	Inside Ourselves
Evil (negative)	Violation by the sins of others	Sin and self-deception
	Evokes degrees of horror, terror, rage, grief, numbness, paralysis	Evokes rationalization, denial, worry, guilt, remorse
	Evil, whether outside or inside us, has the potential to halt our spiritual progress, injure relationships, and distance us from God	

In summary, both evils we commit and those we just experience can distance us from God, drive a wedge between us and other people, and put us at enmity with ourselves. How do we obtain deliverance from these powerful effects of evil?

Submission to the sovereignty of God is the beginning. Thus, a prayer that ends, "deliver us from evil," can *only* begin, "Our Father which art in heaven, Hallowed be thy name. Thy kingdom come. Thy will be done in earth, as it is in heaven" (Matthew 6:9–10). What follows in the remainder of the Lord's Prayer is not a random list of lovely sentiments, but systematic instruction in the assumptions, helps, and responses we need in order to gain deliverance from evil, whether in the world or in us, that we may participate in the righteous kingdom, power, and glory of our Father both now and "forever." To gain this deliverance, we pray for help in meeting our true needs for "daily bread," as discussed in the last chapter; then we forgive our debtors, we seek forgiveness, and we manage thoughtfully our human susceptibility to temptation.

Forgiving Our Debtors

None of us want to spend eternity with people who hurt us. The justice of God assures us that those who trespass against us will feel personally the impact their sins have had upon us, paying the full penalty for their sins if they do not then sincerely repent (see Doctrine and Covenants 19:15–17). We can be confident in the absolute justice of God, without which He would cease to be God: "What, do ye suppose that mercy can rob justice? I say unto you, Nay; not one whit. If so, God would cease to be God" (Alma 42:25).

God has no tolerance for the ways in which we hurt one another. As an example, noting that the people of Noah's day are "without affection, and . . . hate their own blood," God says, "the fire of mine indignation is kindled against them, and in my hot displeasure will I send in the floods upon them, for my fierce anger is kindled against them" (Moses 7:33–34).

So why in the world does God ask us to "forgive our debtors," even telling us, "he that forgiveth not his brother his trespasses standeth condemned before the Lord; for there remaineth in him the greater sin" (Doctrine and Covenants 64:9). Why can't we have hot displeasure and fierce anger and send in floods upon them too?

Well, we can, for a time (except maybe the sending in floods part). But the teachings of Jesus Christ alone deliver us from evil— the evil out there, and the evil that gets in us when we are affected by the evil out there. We clearly see what lies at the end of the road of vengeance and hatred in the tragic story of Tom above—a good man perpetrating on others the very evils perpetrated upon him, and worse, then left holding the bag of a burden of guilt he cannot set down. That is not a road we want to start down. There is no peace or freedom for us there.

So when evil robs us of our most basic birthright of affection, safety, confidence, trust, and much more, how do we get repaid? To simply forgive those in debt to us is the equivalent of saying, "You don't owe me anymore." But why would we say that?

Because working diligently to forgive the debts owed to us helps us get free from evil that alienates us from ourselves, others, and God.

Georgia recently lost her mother. But Georgia isn't grieving; Georgia is angry. Sure, she is relieved to be freed from the abusive, punishing, deceitful way her mother treated her over a lifetime. But she is also angry to realize that now there will never be an apology, a recognition of wrong, an effort to make up for the harm caused. What kind of a God would expect Georgia to forgive such a debt?

A God who loves her very much. This is how it works:

Georgia's mother cannot pay the debt she owes, even if she wants to, and there is no particular reason to think she even wants to. She does not have the power to turn back the clock and restore Georgia's childhood, grant her the peace and confidence that was destroyed, or make her feel safe. No matter how accurately Georgia asserts, "But you owe me," if Georgia has to wait for her mother to make things right, she will wait forever.

The God whose fiery indignation is kindled by those who are without affection and hate their own blood requires that Georgia's note be repaid, however. In fact, He takes it upon Himself to repay that debt. He promises to pay the debt in full because of His infinite love for Georgia, His precious daughter. However, Georgia must sign over the note to Him. She cannot continue to demand that her mother pay it off if God is going to pay it off. That would not be just. She has to choose: continue to do everything in her power to get her mother to pay the debt, or turn the debt over to God. The latter will mean she must be willing to see the ways God blesses her despite the losses she has incurred—and to trust that in both this life and the next He can continue to pay down that debt until it is paid in "good measure, pressed down, and shaken together, and running over" (Luke 6:38). Given that her mother is completely incapable of paying the debt at all at this point, this is a great trade-off.

But what about Georgia's mother? Does she just get off scot-free? Of course not. She doesn't owe Georgia anymore, but she owes someone. She owes Christ, who earned the right to extend His mercy only by experiencing in Gethsemane every heartache Georgia endured at her mother's hand. Justice would require that *she* suffer every pain she inflicted on Georgia and on the Savior, that she endure every indignation, every humiliation and sorrow, every consequence of her neglect and betrayal of her daughter. If she does not repent, she will still have to suffer in this way. But if she is willing to learn from her mistakes and sins, acknowledge them fully, repent, change her mind, and do all in her power to make things right and to change, then Christ can help her. He can say to Georgia, in essence:

> I'm asking you to set your mother free from the prison she is in, not through any worthiness of hers, but out of love for me. I have fully suffered with you every consequence of your mother's mistreatment. I have walked with you through every heartache. I know precisely and personally every tear you have shed, every fear that has shaken you, every injury you have sustained. I am deeply, personally sorry for what you've undergone.
>
> Although unseen angels invisibly protected and comforted you in some of those experiences, I submitted to them in full, so I have learned by my own experience a level

of compassion and respect for you that you do not even have for yourself. I give you my personal guarantee on the note she owes, and I will fully repay you if you release her to me.

I also know the sins others committed against your mother and the mortal weaknesses she was subject to. I know these, also, in my very pores. I can help you grow enough to have compassion on your mother so you can see—beyond the tyrant you experience—the broken, troubled child at the heart of her sin.

What's more, I will help you repay the debts you owe to those you have hurt with your sins if you are willing to learn from your mistakes and repent.

Then you will be truly free. (See 2 Nephi 2:26)

Georgia has a difficult choice to make, one that may take her years to fully implement. It may take longer than this life, in fact, for her to fully understand and forgive. But asking her to forgive is not the wishy-washy plea of a God who doesn't have the guts to stand up for what is right. Nor is it a tyrannical repeat of her mother's insistence that she is right and Georgia wrong. It is a path to freedom and peace.

S. Michael Wilcox reminded us in a Time Out for Women talk that even if we have not managed to fully repent of every little sin before the Day of Judgment, we can fully cancel all the debts owed to us. What a wonderful feeling it would be to say to the Savior on that day, "No one owes me anything. I have forgiven all. Now please, dear Lord, forgive me."[7]

Forgive Us Our Debts

Our sins may or may not be as grievous as those committed against us, but we all know we need forgiveness as well. I don't pretend to fully understand how Tom, the Vietnam vet, could have taken a different road that horrible day after his closest friend was shot down. In his rage, fear, and grief, and in his role as a soldier, it would certainly have been very, very difficult to choose love and forgiveness over hate and fear. If he were to succeed at such a choice, he would probably need at least the following:

+ the opportunity to put words to his unspeakable story of impotence and loss
+ the chance to have his story received with compassion and empathy
+ a clear understanding of God's justice, love, and mercy
+ the support and skill of a caring religious leader, friend, or mental health professional
+ time to be still and to think before acting
+ reminders of his deepest values and the values of his deceased friend
+ skills for soothing his mind and body
+ patience with himself and from others
+ a chance to grieve fully, surrounded by empathy and love
+ the help of heaven

It would require facing his grief to a degree I can barely contemplate to take this difficult road. But the road he took instead cost him not only his friend but himself and his future. Even more searing than the pain he experienced in the rice paddy the day of the ambush, even worse than the flashbacks that lasso his present back into that past, is the hell he endlessly relives, remembering his own brutality. As hard as it is to forgive those whose evil surrounds us, it is even harder to forgive ourselves when their evil gets inside us.

Tom is not without hope of peace, however. The very resources listed above that could have helped him respond differently to his loss years ago could also help him respond differently now. We can add to those resources additional helps we learn in the gospel of Jesus Christ: restitution, priesthood blessings, and reliance on the Atonement of Jesus Christ. Though I am clearly not the judge who will determine Tom's eternal fate, I do know mutual forgiveness for even horrific sin is possible when both parties can feel themselves held in the arms of the Savior. I can imagine a day when soldiers on both sides of a horrible conflict can find not only resurrection but peace if they can see one another through the eyes of Christ as they share their stories.

Restitution is a powerful gift to help us out of the hell of facing our own capacity for sin. I will never forget the brief but life-changing scene in the movie *Gandhi* (1982), in which a wild-eyed Hindu man bursts into the sanctity of Gandhi's long fast for peace between Hindus and Muslims. The man throws a piece of bread at Gandhi, also a Hindu, and cries out, "Eat! Eat! I am going to hell, but not with your death on my soul!" Gandhi replies that only God decides who goes to hell, but the man gives the tortured reply, "I have killed a child! . . . They killed my son! The Muslims killed my son!"

With measured breath, Gandhi replies, "I know a way out of hell. Find a child—a child whose mother and father have been killed—and raise him as your own. Only be sure that he is a Muslim, and that you raise him as one."[8]

When Gandhi helps this man find a means of making what restitution he can for his sin, he shows him the road out of hell. Even when our sins are far less grievous, you and I must also take that road. It is the road of repentance, restitution, and reliance on the blood of Christ to pay our debts. We may gain access to Christ's fathomless repository when we are willing, as was this Hindu father, to acknowledge our participation in the evil and suffering from which we long to be set free, to do what we can to restore the debts we have incurred, and to grant others the forgiveness we long for.

Even when the horrific effects of evil put us at enmity with ourselves, with others, and with God, Christ has given us a way out of hell.

"Grace Is Sufficient"

Even when our sins are minor compared to those described above, we can struggle to let go of our self-recrimination and accept the Atonement as sufficient for us (see 2 Corinthians 12:9).

One January I received a list of twenty ways to declutter my life for the New Year. That sounded sort of fun, so I opened the list and read the first item: *Let go of a grudge.* I couldn't think of anyone I held a grudge against, so I moved on to more concrete ways of decluttering. But the next day when I decided to come back to the list, I felt a quiet nudge to start again at the top. Again I read, *let go of a grudge.* Hmm. I scanned a mental list of people I had held grudges against in the past, but all seemed resolved. No one else came to mind. But something held me there, thinking about this injunction.

I asked the Lord for help. *Whom do I hold a grudge against?* Into my mind came a single word: *You.*

Hmmm. Me. Well. Yes. I suppose I do hold such a grudge. But I've tried long and hard to release the debts some part of me still thinks some other part of me owes for having been stupid or blind or worse. I've counseled with dozens, maybe hundreds of people to help them forgive themselves. But my own sins and failings still haunt me. I still hate knowing they will always be part of my life story.

Then something caught my attention, something about the quality of this voice that said *You* in my mind. Whose voice was that, anyway? No sooner had I asked the question than I realized it was my mother's voice, my mother who had passed away a year before. I found myself saying, *Okay, Mom, you're right. I do hold that grudge. But I don't know what more I can do about that. I've tried. For years. I know this grudge isn't helpful. But I'm stuck.*

In my mind, I could hear my mother's voice whisper, *Sweetheart, all the people here who love you most know everything about you. We're not shocked or horrified. This is just life. We love you. You learned this hopeless self-disdain from me, and I'm here to tell you I was wrong. Let it go.*

Only God decides who goes to hell, or whose inevitable sentence is commuted because of sincere and complete repentance. In reality, we cannot just choose to forgive ourselves, freeing ourselves from our debts to others. But we can choose to accept the freedom from hell God offers us when He unlocks the door and sets us free. The choice to walk out of hell and let go of our grudges against ourselves is a choice some of us must make again and again. If we have done what we can to renounce our sins, make restitution, forgive others, and learn from our errors, then God has promised His forgiveness. Even if we feel otherwise, we are clean. We get to choose to believe.

I have to assume the blessings Joseph Smith gave to others are canonized in the Doctrine and Covenants only when they have application for more than the individual who received them. Section 108 is such a section. In it the Lord invites us to receive His forgiveness without resistance. If you are one who struggles to let go of sins you've thoroughly repented of, read His words to you:

> Verily thus saith the Lord unto you, my servant . . . : Your sins are forgiven you, because you have obeyed my voice in coming up hither this morning to receive counsel of him whom I have appointed. Therefore, *let your soul be at rest concerning your spiritual standing, and resist no more my voice.* (Doctrine and Covenants 108:1–2; emphasis added)

When we struggle to let go of the grudges we hold against ourselves, we may need to label that struggle for what it is: holding out for some miraculous undoing of our past instead of the miraculous forgiveness we've been given. We're not seeing an accurate portrayal of our dismal spiritual standing before God; we are just being tempted with pride or faithlessness or despair, temptations we can resist. We may need help and tools for dealing with these new temptations, but we don't need more rounds of remorse for old sins. I will talk more about how we can respond to such temptations later in this chapter.

The Impact of Mortal Weakness

Evil is not the only force in the world that has the potential to drive a wedge between us and the Lord, however. Becoming mortal includes being subject to the weakness inherent in our condition here, both because we live in fallen bodies and because we live in a fallen world. Being fallen and weak is not in itself evil; rather, our fallen nature is a neutral condition. But in our weakness, we can struggle to let God close.

I've written about the differences between sin and weakness elsewhere.[9] Because it is so easy for us to miss this distinction, and because there are some serious consequences for doing so, let's note some of the key differences between sin and weakness. First, a quick review of sin—see if you agree:

- Sin is a choice we make to violate our values and the commandments of God we've been taught.
- Depending on our training and accountability, what is a sin for one person may not be a sin for another.
- The results of sin include harm to ourselves and others and distance from God.
- Ultimately, sin leads to eternal death and dismissal from the presence of God unless we repent (changing our mind, behavior, and heart), rely on the Atonement of Christ, and obtain forgiveness.

- When we sincerely repent, God forgives us, returning us to a state of moral cleanliness.
- Satan is the author of sin. He deceives us, encourages self-deception, and tempts us to sin.
- In contrast, Christ decries sin and was completely without sin.

The importance of repentance in response to sin cannot be overemphasized. Repentance includes recognizing and acknowledging our sin, changing our minds about its desirability and efficacy, turning away from sin, making restitution where possible, apologizing to those we have sinned against, and confessing serious sin to appropriate Church leaders who can help us complete our repentance. When we sincerely repent, the Atonement of Christ allows us to be forgiven and clean again. If the forgiveness of those we have wronged takes longer, we are patient, nonjudgmental, humble, and apologetic. But when we have sincerely done all we can to repent and repay, God forgives, and we are clean.

Keep these descriptions of sin in mind now as we look more carefully at weakness—a less familiar concept for most of us. We tend to think of weakness as Sin Lite. But a careful study of the scriptures suggests a different picture of weakness. Misunderstanding that difference can lead us to despair over weakness that is actually a gift from God. The Lord teaches Moroni: *"I give unto men weakness that they may be humble; and my grace is sufficient for all men that humble themselves before me; for if they humble themselves before me, and have faith in me, then will I make weak things become strong unto them"* (Ether 12:27).

Other words for weakness are *infirmity* or *limitation*. So the weakness we are born with can include limitations inherent in the mortal condition such as:

- the inevitability of decline and death
- physical or emotional illness

+ predispositions we are born with to such things as distractibility, anxiety, addiction, or same-sex attraction
+ emotions of all kinds, including anger, fear, shame, and depression
+ limits on our knowledge, skill, stamina, or energy
+ misunderstanding or ignorance due to our limited experience or history
+ the impact of trauma or injury on our development or options
+ susceptibility to temptation

While these are not always pleasant aspects of mortality, they are not sins. Weakness is basically neutral. Satan is eager to play upon our weakness to drag us from neutral over to evil. But God has other purposes for giving us mortal weakness. He wants to use our weakness, the weakness of others, and even the weakness of the earth to make us stronger, wiser, and better. As we humbly exercise our agency in response to such weakness, relying on the grace or enabling power of Christ, we can grow, learn, and become resilient. If we can respond to others' weakness by being calm, curious, and compassionate, we move toward the virtues of reverence, gratitude, mercy, and love. These virtues emerge, however, only if we are humble and have faith in Christ.

Distinguishing our sins from our weakness is not always straightforward, but it helps to try. If we rationalize and justify sin as merely a weakness, we will not repent as we must in order to be clean. By contrast, if we assume our weaknesses are sins, we can become demoralized to the point of giving up because we feel the impossibility of overcoming weakness by willpower alone. Some of the problems of life have elements of both sin and weakness, so we must pray, ponder, and perhaps consult with others to help us distinguish them.

While we can be clean from sin right now, right here, we can't just change our minds and renounce our weakness. In fact, human weakness will always be with us. We will always be limited, inadequate, subject to temptation and error, and influenced by at least some of our history and predispositions. We need to be humble, teachable, and even apologetic for our weakness as we learn coping skills, practice discipline, make plans, practice, exercise patience, pray, ask for support, try not to bug other people, and do our best to learn, not hide. But weakness in itself does not make us unclean.

Christ joins us fully in the mortal condition of human weakness: as a mortal, He too was subject to death, suffering, illness, hunger, thirst, emotions of all kinds, imperfect parents, unkind playmates, impatient teachers, jealous siblings, the need to work for a living, hostile elements, limitations on His energy and capacity, and temptations of every sort. Through experience with His mortal limitations, He increased in compassion, wisdom, and perfect empathy for us.

Four crucial differences between sin and weakness thus emerge:

1. Satan wants us to sin, while God absolutely does not. Yet God gives us weakness.

2. Christ was without sin, but He joins us fully in the state of mortal weakness.

3. We must repent (change our minds, behavior, and hearts) to gain forgiveness from sin and be clean again. But we can't just change our minds about being weak.

4. Sin will destroy us, but when we work humbly and faithfully at our weakness, God can turn it to strength and virtue—especially the godly virtues of compassion, faith, wisdom, patience, charity, integrity, and hope.

We can add *weakness* and *holiness* to the chart begun above, as shown on the following page.

	Outside Ourselves	Inside Ourselves
Evil (negative)	Violation by the sins of others	Sin and self-deception
	Evokes degrees of horror, terror, rage, grief, numbness, paralysis	Evokes rationalization, denial, worry, guilt, remorse
	Evil, whether outside or inside us, has the potential to halt our spiritual progress, injure relationships, and distance us from God	

	Outside Ourselves	Inside Ourselves
Weakness (neutral)	Exposure to others' weakness, or weakness in the earth itself	Experiencing weakness in our mortal body: limitations, emotions, predispositions, illness, personal history, faulty learning, ability to be tempted
	May evoke pity, envy, disdain, indifference, OR curiosity, compassion, generosity	May evoke fear, shame, rationalization, defensiveness, OR humility, learning, resilience
	Weakness can lead us toward either sin (above) OR increased virtue, improved relationships, and greater trust in God (below)	

	Outside Ourselves	Inside Ourselves
Holy strengths (positive)	Exposure to others' holiness inspires and instructs us	Choosing humility and faith in Christ turns weakness to holy strengths of wisdom, charity, and righteous influence
	Evokes feelings of respect, gratitude, love, righteous desire	Evokes feelings of compassion, peace, joy, patience, confidence
	Holiness, whether outside or inside us, has the potential to promote spiritual progress, solidify Zion relationships, and unite us with God	

Prepare Against Temptation

The Lord's essay on weakness in Ether 12:27 portrays humility and faith in Christ as the remedies for human weakness, including our susceptibility to temptation. Managing temptation is crucial if we want to keep weakness from becoming sin and to foster loving, trust-filled relationships with God and other people.

Consistent with the assurance that God does not tempt us or suffer us to be tempted beyond what we can bear (see James 1:13; 1 Corinthians 10:13), Joseph Smith changed the biblical version of the Lord's Prayer slightly to read, "suffer us not to be led into temptation" (JST, Matthew 6:14). Prayer is a commitment to action. When we pray that we won't be led into temptation, we commit not to lead ourselves there either. We recognize that we are not above being tempted, and we also refuse the shame-filled hiding that prevents us from getting help or support in avoiding sin.

When we acknowledge, rather than deny or make excuses for, our human weakness, we recognize we need a plan for managing temptation. We avoid tempting situations where possible, acknowledge what tempts us, distract ourselves from temptation, get support from others, and fast and pray for support from the Spirit. That plan can include not letting ourselves get too hungry (that *daily bread* again), or too tired, bored, stressed, or lonely. The *daily bread* we need includes spiritual closeness and direction, loving connections, exercise and rest, and meaningful work and service— not just physical sustenance. When we ignore any of these human limitations, we are more susceptible to temptation.

While guilt or godly sorrow helps us repent, shame about our weakness does not. Instead of prompting us to repent and make things right, shame prompts us to hide, worry about what others will think, and despair. In contrast, *real* humility helps us acknowledge our weakness and vulnerability to temptation so we can avoid, flee, or overcome it through practice and learning.

When the full-time missionaries received tablets, cell phones, and Facebook access to help them with their work, many struggled with the temptation to use media unwisely, accessing inappropriate content or wasting time. The Church provided counsel, safeguards, and helps for creating a plan for managing those temptations. Adapted to our concerns, these ideas can help us manage our temptations as well:

1. *Be in tune with spiritual promptings.* Pray and ponder about how you can avoid temptation, and heed warnings from the Holy Ghost.

2. *Stay focused on your purpose.* Don't walk into potentially tempting situations (such as turning on a computer) without a clear intention and purpose in mind.

3. *Be aware and acknowledge* when you're feeling vulnerable to temptation. Determine what situations or feelings may increase your vulnerability. Talk about it. Invite support and ideas.

4. *Choose to act.* Get up and move, walk, or change your setting. Recite helpful scriptures or hymns. Take deep breaths to relax and refocus. Remember sweet spiritual experiences. Write down things you're grateful for. Take a break, get some food, get some rest, or exercise. Pray. Get support from others.

5. *Learn and improve.* Make a note of things that work. Notice patterns of when you struggle. Notice and learn from the outcomes of mistakes. Learn, adjust your plan, and improve.

When we recognize our susceptibility to temptation, make plans, invite help, and learn from mistakes, the Lord will help us. Missionaries learn that managing technology wisely is not an individual matter. Mutual support, not shame, is key. Caring support, compassion for ourselves, individual responsibility, and heavenly help can truly "foil the tempter's power."[10]

As a Man Thinketh

One of the biggest temptations faced by scrupulous people is that of not "controlling" our thoughts. When Jesus equates lust with adultery, we might mistakenly assume that a lustful thought is a sin next to murder in seriousness. We may forget that the ability to be *tempted* with lust is a weakness that is part of the mortal condition for each of us, but that being *tempted* is not the same as *giving in* to temptation, courting temptation, or dwelling on temptation. Being tempted with pride is not the same as being prideful. Being tempted to be jealous is not the same as being jealous. Being tempted to hold a grudge is not the same as holding a grudge. Can you feel the difference?

Sometimes trying to control our thoughts feels simply impossible. How many times in the last minute have you thought about a pink elephant? Probably none. Now, get out your watch. For the next minute, don't think about a pink elephant. Control those thoughts! No pink elephants!

The more you try not to think about a pink elephant, the more the pink elephants multiply. And the more emotion you invest in shaming or blaming yourself for thinking of pink elephants, or the more you fear a pink elephant will show up in your mind, the more likely it becomes that you will think of little else. Should you be moderately successful at resisting pink-elephant thoughts for a minute, they would rebound with a vengeance as soon as the minute was over.

So how do you not think about a pink elephant? More successful strategies include:

- Distance: don't look up pink elephants on the Internet, don't review in your mind what a pink elephant would look like, don't dwell on pink elephants you've seen, don't put pink elephants in your snack drawer.
- Detach: make it as unalarming and unshameful as possible any time you actually do think about a pink elephant. (Yawn.)
- Pact and Distract: Get involved with people (pact) in something else (distract). Engage in a meaningful conversation; go to a movie with your sister; walk the dog with your neighbor; go to the grocery store and ask the produce manager about apples.

Distance. Detach. Pact and Distract.

Lust is not the only temptation we have better luck avoiding if we don't get too anxious about avoiding it. The temptation to feel ashamed is another, including the temptation to feel ashamed of our sins or weaknesses, or even ashamed of our struggle to accept God's forgiveness. We can feel tempted to dwell on the sins of others, rehearsing our reasons for not forgiving. We can be tempted by spiritual doubts, worry about the future, or suicidal thoughts. Distance, detach, and pact and distract are good strategies for all of these temptations.

The Antidote to Evil

When I read the Lord's Prayer, I don't just read the words He prays; I also read between the lines to see Christ's humble compassion for us and our human condition. When evil estranges us from ourselves, from other people, and from God, compassion is the antidote.

You may remember my encounter with Christ's compassion when I lost an important computer file some years ago. I was completely distraught about the loss, but I also felt ashamed of making such a fuss about something that, in the big scheme of things, was pretty small potatoes. But when I invited God to simply sit with me and give me courage to redo the lost work, what I felt first, and clearly, was Christ's compassion. Instead of feeling the chiding I expected for making a mountain out of a molehill, I felt, "This *is* hard. I understand. I'm so sorry." My Savior's compassion and humble empathy with my trivial earthly problem gave me compassion for myself as well, helping me turn away from self-pity or rage and grow instead. I have wondered why He didn't just assure me that all would be fine, the file would be found, and there was no cause for alarm. But Christ didn't just assure Mary and Martha that all would be fine and that there was no cause for alarm when Lazarus died, either. Instead, He wept (see John 11:21–35).

From His vast perspective, God always knows that ultimately there is no cause for alarm. Everything will be fine. All of our losses will be made up. All of our injuries will be healed. And yet, He weeps with us. I stand all amazed at such love.

Getting to Holiness

Writing a subtitle about "getting to holiness" makes me sort of cringe. I'm anything but holy. But holiness is not an attribute I either possess or I don't. Holiness is a process I engage in every day as I forgive a debt, overcome a temptation, change my mind about a sin, try again to set down an old worldview, or get a little better at love. I can get pretty discouraged at how often I circle in the same old orbits when I want to head off to the stars, freed from the gravity of evil.

Nathan writes:

> I feel especially loved and close to God right now. Because of my studies over the years, I have more confident impressions that the direction in which I am heading in is in harmony with the direction God wants me to pursue.

When I pray for some of the most glorious blessings, I often get some of the most severe temptations I have ever experienced. Occasionally, I am not as faithful in controlling my temper or thoughts or behavior as I should be. I have come to understand that these bouts are the Lord showing me exactly what I have to work on in preparation for the blessings I seek.

Temptation no longer sends me into spirals of depression or into a giving up attitude. Rather it's a powerful tool of leverage not only to bless my life but to open doors to heavenly light. It is as though I am being carefully tutored through a maze of imperfections of the world, only to come out in the end to a glorious field of blessings I seek. I feel the blessings of the Atonement intensely, more meekness and humility before my Savior, and gratitude beyond anything I can put in words. I feel like I am in His hands, He who purchased me with His blood.[11]

I feel privileged to have learned from and with people like Nathan that:

+ Receiving God's compassion for me in my weakness does more than anything else to help me want to try again.
+ Receiving His compassion for me in my sin does more than anything else to help me want to repent.
+ Receiving His compassion for me when I've been injured does more than anything else to help me want to be compassionate with others.

And from this I conclude: Christ's charitable compassion, His willingness to know me and to love me anyway—this is ultimately what delivers me from evil. This is what makes me truly free.

Chapter 9

LETTING GOD LOVE US

*And we have known and believed the
love that God hath to us.*

(1 John 4:16)

We read, we hear, and it is sweet to imagine that God loves us. We like the images of people partaking of the delicious white fruit of the tree of life. It would probably be exciting to hear an angelic chorus sing in triumph: *"For thine is the kingdom, and the power, and the glory, for ever. Amen!"* (Matthew 6:13). But do we believe that love, that fruit, that power and glory are really for us? Not always. When we don't, it is easy to assume that God needs to do something to convince us. But as the angels repeatedly make clear in their interactions with mortals, the choice to receive that love, partake of that fruit, and participate in that glorious power and kingdom is not one He can make for us. We must choose to receive. We must choose to believe.

Why We Don't

This book began with the simple question, "Why do we keep God so far away?" Let's review some of the reasons we might not let God's love in, preferring instead to keep God at a distance:

1. We're going through a stage. We may keep Him far away because our relationship with God, like all relationships, goes through many stages. Although in some of those stages we feel close to Him, in others we back away. When we're angry or confused, we may wrestle with the Lord as we try to work things out. Or we may create distance, hoping that with time we'll get a new perspective that will allow us to reconnect on new terms. Ironically, we often engage in power struggles or withdraw in order to *keep the relationship alive* even if it doesn't feel especially close at the moment.

2. We've been burned in the past. We may keep God far away because we have been disappointed, neglected, or hurt by love, and we don't want a repeat. We may not know what healthy love is supposed to look like. We've learned instead to cling anxiously in fear of abandonment or rejection, not really trusting God or seeing Him for who He is. Or we keep God away because we keep everyone away; love feels like a risk that is simply too dangerous to take.

3. We're afraid He's out to get us. We may keep our distance from God as a way to keep our distance from a future that He prophesies and that we fear. We may worry that if we signal our desire to be close, God will decide we need more adversity first. Or that if we have a deep spiritual experience, unbearable trials will follow. We worry God will throw some huge Abrahamic test our way, taking our children or ruining our lives to see if we'll stay faithful. We try to stay close enough to placate God, but not so close as to make Him think He'd better start pushing us harder. We misunderstand who God is.

4. We're too hungry to hold still. We may keep God far away because our present hungers keep us scrambling and we don't stop to cultivate stillness and invite Him near. We keep ourselves too busy, too preoccupied with our lists and self-expectations to soak in beauty, ponder blessings, or overflow with gratitude. In our efforts to either ignore our hunger or control and hoard supplies, we're afraid to trust that God will give us today's bread today if we slow down enough to feel how keenly we want to sup with Him.

5. *We think He owes us, or we owe Him.* We may keep God far away because we feel angry about evil and injustice we think God is responsible for, or we may be drawn away from God by the temptations of the world. Our weakness, sin, and struggles to forgive may leave us feeling ashamed and unworthy of closeness, or defensive and resistant to it. We may be afraid that we'll never get what we're owed if we forgive, or that we owe too much to ever be forgiven. We don't realize that God is the only one who can repay us for the debts we're owed and the only one who can fully pay off our debts to others, opening the doors to peace.

These reasons and probably many others can keep us holding God at arm's length, even when we assume He is the one staying away. So let's review a few answers to the even more important question: How can we get better at letting God's love in?

How We Can

1. *Remember God wants to be close to us.* In fact, He goes out on a limb to claim His love for us, to commit to us, and to ask us to be His partner for eternity. We don't need to worry that our longing for Him is too much or that He'd prefer we leave Him alone. He loves us with the tender, delighted, consuming love of a father for his child or a groom for his bride. *We* go through stages that include power struggles and withdrawal on our path to a mature and committed love, but *He* is already fully committed to us. His ways are still not our ways, and we will not always understand why He is silent or doesn't give us our desire. But He has thrown Himself heart and soul into a match made in heaven as He vies for our love

and trust. Now we have to choose again and again through all the inevitable periods of struggle and distance to trust Him as much as He has trusted us. He waits, ever patient, for our response.

As He prayed for His ancient disciples, Christ prays for us, by name. No matter how dark things get, He prays that we will remember the hours He has been with us, feeding us, teaching us, healing us, and promising to return. He is our Advocate, the One who is always on our side. If the voice in our mind is His voice, it will always be gentle, persuasive, humble, non-shaming, and kind, even when He calls us to repent. He is with us in this hour as well, here, today.

We are the children of Israel (Jacob), the man who wrestled with God for His promises to be fulfilled. Belief is not what is left when all the other options have been neatly disposed of, but a choice we make to claim the evidences we have received as sufficient, even in the midst of uncertainty.

2. Relearn what love really means. Our earliest experiences with attachment can leave us secure and prepared to love, or they can leave us anxious, avoidant, ambivalent, or traumatized about love. Without always knowing exactly how, we bring those old templates to our future relationships, including with God. Especially when our early experiences have left us love-hungry and love-injured, we may conclude that love really means starvation, force, indifference, chaos, or pain. We must leave behind our faulty assumptions about ourselves and about love in order to claim God as our Father and grow up again in Him.

Learning to tell our story from a bigger perspective and with more compassion for ourselves and others opens up new options and helps us change our expectations. As we gradually learn to see our parents as just fellow mortals, or sometimes as wounded children, the past loses some of its power to control our present.

Some of our beliefs about what love should be are idealized fantasies of a love so perfect it would make us effortlessly whole, happy, selfless, and spiritually in tune. Instead, we need to work on being more open, vulnerable, accepting, and generous in real human relationships with ordinary mortals in order to grow in our capacity to love. Only then can we prepare for genuine closeness with the God who is patient and compassionate with our weakness.

3. *Practice trusting both God and our own resilience.* Mortality is hard, whether we distance ourselves from God or live righteously. But things don't just get worse for us because God peevishly starts looking for ways to test us the minute we decide to be good. Some of our mortal challenges are things we wanted to experience and signed up for before we came here, and God keeps His covenants with us to allow us these experiences even when they no longer seem like a good idea to us. Other things happen as a result of our poor choices or the choices of others, and God promises He can fully redeem these things if we turn to Him. But we don't need to fear that if we try to claim the promises of Abraham, God will up the ante by making our lives miserable.

We can soothe our anxiety about the future God has in store by making sure the image of God we hold when we pray is consistent with who God really is: merciful, good, wise, kind, patient, strong, and humble. We can feed feelings of security and safety and try not to get anxious about being anxious. We can choose to trust our own resilience, rather than putting all our effort into making sure God will keep us safe. And we can look for the ways God has already turned the straw and refuse of our lives into the gold of wisdom, character, charity, and other priceless gifts, remembering that He will surely continue to do so.

4. *Sit at the cookfire of Christ.* The companionship of the Spirit is our most pressing need. When we sit, center, and invite God

close, He will come. With practice, we can develop eyes to see and hearts to feel His presence, even when we are busy with the necessary work of this world. He can show us where the fish are so we do not labor in vain. Not only can He fix us spiritual breakfast and guide us to fulfill our missions, but He can teach us about love and make us equal to all that loving ourselves, others, and God requires from us.

5. *Repent, forgive, and let go.* Though we live in the constant presence of evil, we can be clean and at peace as we repent and forgive. We don't have to be free from all mortal weakness in order to be clean. It isn't a sin to be tired or discouraged, to grieve or to fear, to get triggered by new reminders of old wounds, to fail at a goal, or to be tempted. Being tempted with evil thoughts is not the same as participating in evil thoughts, and "distance, detach, pact, and distract" works better to help us eschew evil than trying to control and fight it.

Forgiving the debts others owe us does not mean pretending no debt was incurred, but rather turning our debt over to Christ. When we do this, He can repay us what those who robbed us cannot repay. We can also choose to let go of the grudges we hold against ourselves. When we are tempted to hold on to old self-recrimination long after our sincere repentance is complete, we can also remember to "distance, detach, pact, and distract" from the temptation of despair. Christ's charitable compassion is the antidote to evil, and compassion for ourselves and others is the greatest tool we have for being delivered from evil.

Life at the Cookfire

These ideas have all been deeply impactful for me personally or I wouldn't be writing about them. But I can't usually hold more than one or two ideas from any book I read. If you can't either, is there one idea, one image, or one story you want to remember, reflect on, practice, and come back to when it feels hard to let God's love in?

If I had to choose one image it would be of Christ, the risen Lord, sitting with His Apostles in the dirt, feeding them breakfast and talking about love (see John 21:1–17). I believe God wants to sit with us, feed us, love us, and remind us of why we can afford to trust Him. I absolutely believe He can redeem anything He allows to happen to us and turn it to our good. Even when it looks for all the world like God has deserted us and evil has won, as epitomized for Christ's disciples by His death on the cross, God comes back. God always comes back. And He comes with His hands open, full of love.

If we are willing to invite Him to come close, God will not only sit with us, He will walk into the world with us. Of course, the disciples who walked with Christ on the road to Emmaus did not immediately recognize Him, and we may also need practice to notice Him at our side. But when we invite Him, He comes. Our task is to find the cues that will tune us into His presence. Here are some that work for me:

Walk with God. Stanford researchers found that students who walked on a treadmill showed significant, substantial improvements in their performance on a creativity test compared with others who sat still.[1] Going for a walk not only strengthens the body God has given us and puts us in touch with the beauty of His earth, but it opens our mind to fresh insights on problems and fresh options for living well. It's great to get outside in nature, but even walking on a treadmill apparently provides some of these benefits. As I walk with God, He can bring scriptures to my mind, help me think through problems, and join my delight at the wonders of the world.

Eat with God. I can't imagine anyone rushing through that meal on the shores of Galilee with the risen Lord. I'm sure they lingered gratefully over every bite He had prepared for them with His own hands. I have noted that when we partake of the sacrament, we pray that we will *eat in remembrance* of Him. To me this suggests that every meal, every morsel we eat, can be a reminder to me of the Bread of Life, the Living Manna, who offered His life for my sustenance.

One of my colleagues, Carrie Skarda, teaches a wonderful seminar on mindful eating at Sixteen Stones Center for Growth. She points out that when we practice mindfulness it isn't a failure to get distracted. Drifting minds are not only inevitable, they are the barbells of mindfulness training that make us strong as we lift them. Noticing our mind drift and returning to mindful awareness in the moment is how we lift the barbells. Eating mindfully follows this pattern. Eating slowly, deliberately, with attention to the taste, smell, and texture of the food, with awareness of the labor that went into its production, and with gratitude for the plants and animals God has provided to nourish us—all of this can turn ordinary eating into a kind of delighted worship that nourishes both body and soul.

The Lord teaches:

> The fulness of the earth is yours, the beasts of the field and the fowls of the air, and that which climbeth upon the trees and walketh upon the earth;
>
> Yea, and the herb, and the good things which come of the earth, whether for food or for raiment, or for houses, or for barns, or for orchards, or for gardens, or for vineyards;
>
> Yea, all things which come of the earth, in the season thereof, are made for the benefit and the use of man, both to please the eye and to gladden the heart;

Yea, for food and for raiment, for taste and for smell, to strengthen the body and to enliven the soul.

And it pleaseth God that he hath given all these things unto man. (Doctrine and Covenants 59:16–20)

Work with God. Whether I am working at home cleaning the garage or supervising children, in an office or a classroom, bogged down in trivia or pushed to my limit by new problems, I can use work as a reminder to invite Him to help me feel the gratitude of having work to do and the pleasure of organizing, planning, and accomplishing. Inviting Him close, I see better how my work connects me to my highest values and goals, and how I can use work to build relationships that will bless me and others. Christ spent long years as an apprentice and a carpenter. He is not a stranger to work, its challenges and opportunities. He will work with me.

Play with God. Inviting God to play with me as I enjoy creative pursuits, playful interactions with others, restful delights, or the happy laughter of children helps me imagine His smile and His joyful heart. Creativity and playfulness are ideal moments to invite God close, for I practice the Creator's gifts when I play. When He tutors me in the delights of creating with a beginner's mind or a master's skill, I remember His love and companionship.

Go to church with God. While it seems sort of obvious to invite God to join our worship, I seldom think to invite God close when I am sitting through a boring class or an annoying talk. Yet even a dull meeting can be a cue to seek personal revelation and feel God's closeness. As I do, I remember His love for the person presenting, His empathy with my feelings, and His instruction about other concerns I have.

If Jesus came in person to church with us, what would He do? Would He lead the singing, teach Primary, sit in the hall with the teenagers skipping class, or pass the sacrament with the deacons?

How would our experience of such things change if we knew He was the one commenting in class, saying the prayer, or sitting next to us on the pew? He invites us as we partake of the sacrament to remember the hours He has been with us. Can next week's sacrament meeting be one of those hours? If I invite Him, will He not come with me to a meeting where everything is said and done in His name?

Invite God into our conversations. The Lord invites, "when ye are assembled together ye shall instruct and edify each other" (Doctrine and Covenants 43:8). He adds elsewhere, "Therefore, strengthen your brethren in all your conversations, in all your prayers, in all your exhortations, and in all your doings. And behold, and lo, I am with you to bless you and deliver you forever" (Doctrine and Covenants 108:7–8). It seems God is eager for us to invite Him into every conversation and interaction to help us edify and strengthen one another. When I silently invoke His company as I talk with other people, I tune in more deeply, share more honestly, and listen more intently for promptings about how I can encourage, edify, and strengthen others. Conversation, whether trivial or significant, reminds me of God's love for us all.

Pray with God. Obviously we pray *to* God, but what would it be like to also pray *with* Him? There are many ways we can use prayer to remind us to invite God close. One friend of mine imagines Christ kneeling with her, His arm around her, when she prays. As we've already learned, prayer doesn't have to include words: we can simply sit quietly and invite God to sit with us, perhaps writing down what comes up for us as we do. My husband regularly prays to know whom he can help today, and as he acts on promptings they come more frequently and he feels God's love more readily. Praying out loud with a paper and pen in hand helps me stay focused, and impressions come more readily. Reading the scriptures can be a prayerful experience, especially when we write down what we learn, feel, or wonder as we read. When I was in private practice, my over-full calendar became an opportunity for prayer as I turned my day over to God and asked Him to make it work out. I've almost always gotten answers, even if not right away, when I pray for help in knowing my sins or weaknesses, strengths or progress. We have been counseled to pray solely to express gratitude at times, and nightly prayers consisting entirely of telling God our favorite parts of the day send us peacefully to sleep. When the Nephites and Lamanites prayed with Christ, they "did not multiply many words, for it was given unto them what they should pray for, and they were filled with desire" (3 Nephi 19:24).

Becoming Like Him

The more we invite God close, the more we learn to see His hand in all good things. As we become more like Him, His holy attributes become clearer to us, for we can see much better what we have experienced and what we are becoming. We learn day by day to see the face of God—and live.

While members of the Godhead are so united I have made little attempt to distinguish Them here, each has distinctive roles that we can learn from and emulate. What do They each do that we can also experiment with, practice, and develop in ourselves? Joseph Smith taught:

> Everlasting covenant was made between three personages before the organization of this earth and relates to their dispensation of things to men on the earth. These personages . . . are called God the first, the Creator; God the second, the Redeemer; and God the third, the Witness or Testator.[2]

God the Creator, our Heavenly Father, is distinguished by His creative and patriarchal power to engender spiritual life in others. He brings order, beauty, and life out of unorganized matter. We can participate as cocreators with God when we give physical and spiritual life to His children, or when we bring order and beauty out of chaos, including the chaos of our internal worlds. As we grow up in Him, we set down the redundancy and destructive impact of old habits and assumptions, and we create new ways to think, behave, and feel that are filled with light and truth.

As I've written about elsewhere, the temple tutors us in God's creative power and in how we might emulate that power in our small way.[3] We can learn to tolerate the anxiety of going down into the chaos of unorganized matter; to plan, work in stages, and evaluate with the help of others; and to claim the goodness of our creations as they bless others. While His creative work is vast and ours is small, He has a work for each of us to do, and we are born to create:

> Behold, I am the Lord God Almighty, and Endless is my name; for I am without beginning of days or end of years; and is not this endless?
>
> And, behold, thou art my son; wherefore look, and I will show thee the workmanship of mine hands; but not all, for my works are without end, and also my words, for they never cease. . . .
>
> *And I have a work for thee . . . my son;* and thou art in the similitude of mine Only Begotten. (Moses 1:3–4, 6)

God the Redeemer, our Savior Jesus Christ, is the Prince of Peace and King of Righteousness into whose holy priesthood order both men and women enter through temple covenants and ordinances.[4] While the Father's creative role is to bring order and life out of unorganized matter, Christ's redemptive role in the Godhead is to bring holiness out of suffering.

Only in a world of agency can growth and learning occur, but mistakes and sins also bring sorrow and pain. Satan apparently didn't think agency was worth this painful price, and he still tries to convince us that he alone can free us from suffering and fear. (Ironically, God and all the heavens weep over those who follow Satan, because God knows how immeasurably they will suffer.) Christ submitted fully to the plan of agency and suffering, offering redemption to all humankind.

We participate in our small way in Christ's redemptive power when we too submit to God's plan of agency and suffering, when we learn and grow through suffering instead of allowing it to defeat us, and when we respond to suffering by claiming our agency to forgive and to learn. Even in the presence of evil, we can choose the godly attributes of humility, mercy, compassion, wisdom, and love.

We further participate in Christ's redemptive role as our Advocate when we become advocates for others, sacrifice to do for others what they cannot do for themselves, and bolster others' efforts to become holy and strong instead of bitter and resentful as they suffer. Timothy teaches: "For if we be dead with him, we shall also live with him: If we suffer, we shall also reign with him" (2 Timothy 2:11–12).

God the Testator, the Holy Ghost, is distinguished in the Godhead by His witnessing and comforting power. When Alma and his people were baptized, they also covenanted to share burdens, mourn with those who mourn, comfort those who stand in need of comfort, and testify of Christ at all times, in all things, and in all places. This is, in essence, the work of the Holy Ghost.

We learn in the temple both to recognize and to become holy messengers who, like the Holy Ghost, bear record of the Father and the Son, minister to Their children, and teach others Their ways. Now and in eternity, when we speak the words of Christ, we speak with the tongue of angels to help bring people to Christ, especially in our families and among our ancestors and progeny. To do so, we must know Him, love Him, and follow Him. Nephi teaches:

> Do ye not remember that I said unto you that after ye had received the Holy Ghost ye could speak with the tongue of angels? And now, how could ye speak with the tongue of angels save it were by the Holy Ghost?
>
> Angels speak by the power of the Holy Ghost; where-fore, they speak the words of Christ. (2 Nephi 32:2–3)

The restored gospel of Jesus Christ gives us an unprecedented glimpse of the work of eternity, work we can begin here and now as we come to Christ, receive His love, organize our lives according to His laws, receive a fulness of the Holy Ghost, and obtain and fulfill our errands from the Lord. We can be prepared to obtain every needful thing, in both good times and hard times, as we im-merse ourselves in His love and grow up in Him (see Doctrine and Covenants 109:15).

Any Empty Chair

Both as a psychologist working with clients and as a human being trying to get by, I've learned often and deeply just how hard life is. Nobody gets through without setbacks and suffering, in-cluding setbacks that seem insurmountable and suffering that feels unbearable.

Often the circumstances life hands us are not the biggest prob-lem, however. The biggest problem is what we tell ourselves this setback or suffering means about us and about God. If we con-clude our setbacks and suffering mean we are unlovable, unworthy, incompetent, or doomed, then problems leave us anxious, angry, ashamed, and depressed. If we assume our setbacks and suffering mean God doesn't care, isn't paying attention, isn't fair, or isn't around, then problems evoke crises of faith. If we believe a problem is something God can always redeem, that His love for us is perfect and infinite, that He can use any circumstance to enhance our creativity, strengthen our character, deepen our relationships, or mature our spiritual gifts, then our amazing capacity for resilience is engaged by His grace.

What helps some of us respond with spiritual resilience and hope in the face of problems, while others respond with despair? Our mortal bodies, families, and circumstances unfold in almost infinite variety. The agency of other people, individually and collectively, bombards us relentlessly. Our own decisions and choices, informed or blind, open up some paths and shut down others. Premortal agendas and covenants we no longer remember may influence our opportunities, predispositions, limitations, and how much or in what ways God responds. Yet all of our experience with setbacks and suffering can, if we are willing, catapult us into the realm of God's creative, redemptive, and witnessing power.

I have asserted repeatedly in this book my increasingly firm conviction that God does not allow anything to happen to us here that He cannot fully and gloriously redeem. In fact, I believe He promised that to us when He sent us here—and how we must have relied on that promise in making the choice to come! We have to choose to participate in that redemption, which will continue into the spirit world. But I believe God's power to redeem—to bring holiness out of suffering—is as vast and limitless as His power to bring order and beauty out of chaos.

But I can only hold onto these lofty perspectives when I am convinced of and held in God's love. My grasp on that love is too often tenuous, even though He always reaches out to me. I have to work hard to remember and be willing to invite God to sit with me and know me. That level of vulnerability is not easy to maintain.

Practice helps. A simple cue that reminds me of my intention is an empty chair. I try to let any empty chair serve as a reminder of God's desire to be close to me. In a restaurant, in my car, in the temple, at church, in the solitude of my home office, on a park bench, in a classroom or a meeting, empty chairs cue me to invite God to join me in my crazy life, encircle me in the arms of His love, teach me, redeem me, and send me out to serve. You are welcome to borrow my cue, or you may want to find your own. However you choose to do so, I hope you will find some way to notice more often the quiet knock of the Savior at your door and invite Him to sup with you. We truly can have the constant companionship of the Holy Ghost. Our Father, our Abba, though unseen and sometimes unfelt, is always near.

Elder D. Todd Christofferson has written about hearing a radio interview several years ago with Bishop Desmond Tutu, the Anglican archbishop who was heavily involved in South Africa's efforts to heal after the years of apartheid. During the interview, the host asked if Bishop Tutu's relationship with God had changed as he had grown older. Bishop Tutu thoughtfully responded, "Yes. I am learning to shut up more in the presence of God." Instead of a "shopping list" approach to prayer, he said, "I think [I am] trying to grow in just being there. Like when you sit in front of a fire in winter, you are just there in front of the fire, and you don't have to be smart or anything. The fire warms you."[5]

Elder Christofferson comments, "I think that is a lovely metaphor—just sit with the Lord and let Him warm you like a fire in winter. You don't have to be perfect or the greatest person who ever graced the earth or the best of anything to be with Him.

"I hope you will take time . . . to sit for a few quiet moments and let the Savior's Spirit warm you and reassure you of the worthiness of your service, of your offering, of your life. . . . Let that moment be one of rest and refreshing and reassurance and renewal."[6]

My hope echoes that of Elder Christofferson: I hope you will take the risk to let God love you, right now, right here. I know He does.

Appendix

WORKBOOK

Chapter Two

1. Questions for the Honeymoon Stage:
   * When did you fall in love with God?
   * What were your most meaningful spiritual experiences?

2. Questions for the Power Struggle Stage:
   * List ten questions or problems you have had with God over the years.
   * Are there any you've solved or that you think might be solvable? Do any fall into your "69 percent" of problems with God or the Church that are not fully resolvable in this life?

3. Questions for the Withdrawal Stage:
   * What would you have to believe about God in order to hold on despite times of distance or silence with God?
   * What would you need Him to understand about you?

4. Questions for the Acceptance and Renewal Stage:
   * What do you imagine a mature relationship with God would look like or feel like?
   * How would you know if you had it? How would you know if you don't?

Chapter Three

1. Questions for the Precommitment Stage:
   + Why do you want to believe in God? What advantages do you see in choosing to believe?
   + Why don't you? What interferes with your belief? Can you tell Him? (He can take it.)

2. I was taught a simple exercise by Dr. Gary Weaver, a gifted psychotherapist who gave me permission before his untimely death to share it. It takes only a few minutes, and I hope you will try it. It will work best if you put your finger in the book so you can read these statements one at a time, then close your eyes and take time to let yourself imagine your response to each statement before going on to the next one.
   + In a private place where you can feel safe and relaxed, close your eyes, take a few deep breaths, relax your shoulders, and let the tension go out of your body as much as you can. When you're ready, read the next statement.
   + Close your eyes again, and imagine a group of people who have your best interests at heart. They can be young or old, living or dead, people you know intimately or people you have not even met in person. The one thing they must have in common is that you truly believe they have your best interests at heart. Take your time to gather this group. When they are assembled, read the next statement.
   + Close your eyes again, and notice the group of people you have assembled, the ones who have your best interests at heart. Ask the group this question: "Do you love me?" Then receive their response.
   + Close your eyes again, and if you have not already done so, consider inviting God to join this group of people who have

your best interests at heart. Imagine inviting God to join this group.

+ Turn to God and ask: "Do you love me?" Then receive God's response.

+ Ask God and the others, "What could I do to receive your love more fully?" and receive their response.

+ When you are done, take a few minutes to write down what you learned or felt.

3. Because one of my dearest friends lives far away, we write each other emails many times a week to keep up with each other's lives, share our questions and ideas, and express our feelings. When you feel far away from God, writing a prayer may be easier and bring more clarity and closeness than trying to speak. Other alternatives might include such things as dancing, drawing, singing, or woodworking your prayers.

Chapter Four

1. When you are struggling in your relationship with God, what words best describe how God seems to you?

O Indifferent

O Available

O Unfair

O Confusing

O Critical

O Interested

O Disappointed

O Demanding

O Kind

O Blaming

O Helpful

O Rejecting

O Preoccupied

O Concerned

O Absent

O Reaching toward me

O Other: _____

When you experience God this way, how might you respond?

- ○ Pleading with Him
- ○ Withdrawing from or ignoring Him
- ○ Calming or soothing myself
- ○ Getting angry with Him
- ○ Resenting Him
- ○ Getting curious about His perspective
- ○ Staying very busy
- ○ Distracting myself
- ○ Focusing on gratitude
- ○ Whining
- ○ Feeling sad
- ○ Being still
- ○ Feeling worthless
- ○ Blaming myself
- ○ Pondering
- ○ Pushing Him away
- ○ Feeling self-pity
- ○ Remembering times of closeness
- ○ Trying harder
- ○ Feeling ashamed
- ○ Feeling compassionate
- ○ Other: _____

2. What early experiences do these current feelings remind you of? Is there a story or image that comes to mind?

3. Can you remember a time when you were able to be calm, curious, and compassionate in a human relationship? What happened?

4. What would it feel like to imagine that God is calm, curious, and compassionate with you?

5. If you were to have an experience tonight that profoundly convinced you that God is trustworthy with the fallible and imperfect person you are and that He deeply and personally loves you, what would be good about that? How would your life be different?

6. If you had such an experience tonight, what would have to change tomorrow in your beliefs, behavior, self-image, feelings, or relationships? Can you get really specific?

7. What would be bad about having such an experience? I encourage you to think about this question especially seriously. Would you be angry that it hadn't happened sooner? Would you be out of excuses for things you don't like about your life? Would you have to make commitments you can now avoid? Would you feel shame? Fear? More lonely than ever once it was over? What else might be bad about it?

8. If your current view of God includes negative perceptions you suspect may not be accurate, it may help to see those perceptions as temptations to surmount, not truths you either accept or resist. How do you generally cope with temptation? Would those tools be useful here? See chapter 8 for more ideas on dealing with temptation.

Chapter Five

1. I strongly encourage you to write a few things down in answer to the following six questions if you want to gain the considerable insights this exercise can provide. (It will be quite difficult to get the same impact without writing things down.)

Relationship Patterns[1]

a. As you remember some of your best times with your parents (or caretakers), list at least 6–8 positive traits of either of your parents. (Examples: funny, hardworking, forgiving, warm, generous, flexible, bold, responsible.) Circle the three best traits.

b. Thinking back to some of your most painful experiences with your parents (or caretakers), list at least 6–8 negative traits of either of them. (Examples: critical, gone a lot, dishonest, depressed, dangerous, boring, stingy, intrusive.) Circle the three worst traits.

c. What were your deepest fears with any of your parents or caretakers? (Examples: afraid of being neglected, embarrassed, rejected, humiliated, inadequate, invisible, used, dominated, hurt.) Circle the worst fears.

d. What did you want but not get from your parents or caretakers? (Examples: an apology, an explanation of what happened, to feel important and accepted as I am, to feel safe, that she'd take charge of her life, that he'd tell me he loved me.) Circle the deepest unmet desires.

e. As a child relating to your parents or caretakers, what negative feelings or thoughts about yourself did you have over and over? (Feelings like: worried, frustrated, sad, ashamed. Thoughts like: I'm not safe, I'm not good enough, nobody cares about me, I'm stupid.) Circle the worst feelings or thoughts.

f. *In the left column on the chart on page 209:* List three frustrating experiences you had as a child in your home (for example: hating to go to bed, Dad always being late, no one helping me with homework, couldn't have friends over, fights over chores, Mom criticizing my appearance).

In the right column on the chart: For each frustration you listed on the left, write in the right column two ways that you typically responded (for example: argued, sneaked around, felt ashamed, gave up, ignored them and left, complained to friends, cried).

	Left—Frustrations		Right—Responses
(A)		(1)	
		(2)	
(B)		(1)	
		(2)	
(C)		(1)	
		(2)	

To see how your childhood conclusions may be affecting your relationships today, including with God, fill in your answers to the questions that follow, writing in your answers from questions a through f above as explained below.

1. I have unconsciously spent my life searching for a God with these traits (write below the words you circled under question a above):

2. What I tend to both look for and fear are evidences that God is really (write here the words you circled under question b above):

3. I unconsciously expect God to make me feel (write here what you circled under question c above):

4. ...and then I wish God would only give me (write here what you circled under question d above):

5. ...even though unconsciously I don't think He will.

6. When my needs are not met or I am under stress I often feel (write here what you circled for e above):

7. ...and I assume God is responsible for my feelings.

8. Then I often respond this way (write here some of the things you wrote in the *right* column for f above, perhaps at a little more abstract level; for example, if you wrote

for f above "snuck into the attic, then felt sorry for myself"
you might write here "hide and feel sorry for myself"):

9. ... when what I really need to do to heal and grow is the
opposite of this, which would be:

(For example, if you wrote "hide and feel sorry for myself"
above, your answer here might be "come to God directly
and honestly, being compassionate with myself but not
self-pitying." If you're not sure what the *opposite* would be,
you might think and pray about this more, or ask someone else's opinion.)

10. Capture below anything you learned from this exercise
(or just ponder it):

_____

_____

_____

2. Think of an especially difficult experience you had in your childhood, youth, or adulthood.

  ◆ What painful lessons did you learn from this experience?

  ◆ What did you learn from this experience that has made you
a better person?

3. Sitting right where you are, look around at your life. What evidences do you see that God cherishes you and cares for you?

Chapter Six

1. When you pray, begin by making sure the image of God you are
holding is consistent with your deepest trust in who God truly is.

2. Which of the attachment tools in the numbered list on pages
124–29 might work best for you? Read through the list and
choose some tools you can use to deliberately solidify your feelings of secure attachment with the Lord.

3. What are your family stories or personal symbols of resilience, faith, or loving care? Consider compiling some of these stories to reflect on again and again.

Chapter Seven

1. Sit still and invite God close. Pray with paper and pencil in hand, and write down what comes up, or what comes through. Act on impressions to serve. Allow your heart to be open to the possibility that God sits in the "love seat" with you.

2. As you partake of the sacrament, remember the hours Christ has been with you. Savor them again.

3. Taste and see: What evidences of God's love are around you right now? What feeds your soul today?

Chapter Eight

1. When the heartache of worldly evil threatens to overwhelm you, ask the Father to help you understand how He sees all of this differently from how you see it. Something in His perspective allows Him, despite His complete empathy and tears for our suffering, to be a God of patience, love, and joy. What?

2. Asking the Lord to help you distinguish your sins from your weaknesses, take the appropriate action for one of them.

3. Make a plan for dealing with a temptation that commonly befalls you. For example, you might be tempted by despair, shame, fear, disbelief, resistance to prayer, laziness, envy, and so forth.

ACKNOWLEDGMENTS

When trying to receive and learn the lofty gift of charity, it helps to consider the many mundane and still miraculous ways that love takes shape in ordinary life. Learning to receive these as the gifts from God I believe them to be is not always easy, but I wish to acknowledge here at least a few of the many people whose love and kindness have informed my understanding of who God is, who I am, and what the world can be.

I sincerely thank Lisa Roper, editor extraordinaire, Laurel Christensen Day, and Emily Watts at Deseret Book for their skillful shaping and shepherding of this book and for their friendship. Thanks to Shauna Gibby for her beautiful cover and design work, and to Rachael Ward for the typography. I appreciate Chrislyn Woolston and the Time Out for Women production team, presenters, and attendees; BYU students and colleagues, especially Scott Richards, Allen Bergin, and Tim Smith; too many friends and colleagues to name at the Association of Mormon Counselors and Psychotherapists; Richard Ferre, Richard Heaton, David Seamons, Kevin Theriot, others involved in missionary mental health, and a whole lot of missionaries I've been privileged to serve with; and the many clients, friends, and fellow Saints who have allowed me to learn from and share their stories. All of these groups have provided insights, incubators, and forums for the development of these ideas.

At a more personal level, I am especially indebted to Christine Packard and Carrie Skarda, my partners at Sixteen Stones Center for Growth, for their inspiring insights about the gospel and about life, their teaching and organizational skills, their very helpful feedback on early drafts of this book, and their good cooking. I also thank Kathleen Flake, Karen Blake, Nancy Brockbank, and my sister Carla Hickman for teaching me, inspiring me, motivating me, walking with me, and loving me so well. They are eternal friends and true spiritual teachers, each in her own way. I thank my children, Carrie, Monika, and Mike, and their spouses, Michael Skarda, Chris Myers, and Melanie Ulrich, who have taught me not only about resilience and love but about psychology, sociology, gender, business, statistics, humor, writing, politics, teaching, medicine, service, engineering, creativity, faith, parenting, true religion, and the joys of loving grandchildren. I feel incredibly blessed to have children who have also become true colleagues and friends. Finally I thank my husband, Dave Ulrich, who is also my best friend, supporter, mentor, editor, and business partner, and a patient guinea pig in my fledgling attempts to learn and relearn the art of love. *Plus qu'hier, moins que demain.*

For reasons I don't fully understand, I've always been a little uncomfortable when authors thank God in their acknowledgments. I guess it seems like a most flagrant understatement to add His name to those of mere mortals when expressing thanks. Or maybe it seems to claim some special status or endorsement from the divine that I don't wish to claim. But when writing a book about the love of God, it feels ridiculous to gloss over my appreciation for God's sustaining love just because that love is both obvious and universal. So I acknowledge and thank my Father, my Savior Jesus Christ, and the Holy Ghost for the precious gifts of order and agency, sacrifice and redemption, revelation and comfort—manifestations of Their love that I have learned to trust and aspire to emulate.

NOTES

—◦❧✦❧◦—

Chapter 1: Why Is God Far Away?

1. James G. Stokes, "Christ Has Felt My Pain," *Ensign*, July 2015, 27.
2. Quoted in Ardeth G. Kapp, "Encircled in the Arms of His Love," BYU Women's Conference 1999, 3. Address at funeral of Florence Johnson; typescript in Kapp's possession, 27. http://ce.byu.edu/cw/womensconference /pdf/archive/1999/kapp_ardeth.pdf.
2. Boyd K. Packer, "The Plan of Happiness," *Ensign*, May 2015, 28.

Chapter 2: Stages of Committed Relationships

1. Isaac Watts, "My Shepherd Will Supply My Need" (1719).
2. See Sherod Miller, Daniel Wackman, Elam Nunnally, and Phyllis Miller, *Connecting with Self and Others* (Littleton, CO: Interpersonal Communications Programs, 1988).
3. Packer, "The Plan of Happiness," 26.
4. Harville Hendrix, *Getting the Love You Want: A Guide for Couples*, 20th Anniversary edition (New York: Henry Holt, 2007); Sue Johnson, *Hold Me Tight: Seven Conversations for a Lifetime of Love* (New York: Little, Brown and Co., 2008).
5. John M. Gottman and Nan Silver, *The Seven Principles for Making Marriage Work* (New York: Three Rivers Press, 1999), 130–31.
6. Packer, "Plan of Happiness," 26.
7. History, circa Summer 1832, The Joseph Smith Papers, accessed 23 Oct. 2015, http://josephsmithpapers.org/paperSummary/history-circa -summer-1832&p=3.
8. Anonymous, personal correspondence.

Chapter 4: Discovering Our Relationship Assumptions

1. Anonymous, personal correspondence.
2. See John Bowlby, *Attachment and Loss—Volume 1: Attachment* (New York: Basic Books, 1969).
3. Mary Ainsworth and John Bowlby, *Child Care and the Growth of Love* (London: Penguin Books, 1953).
4. See, for example, Tim Clinton and Joshua Straub, *God Attachment: Why You Believe, Act, and Feel the Way You Do about God* (New York: Howard Books, 2010).
5. Researchers have titled and defined these styles in different ways over decades of research; the notion of discrete categories is not considered essential to Bowlby's theory.
6. See Bessel Van der Kolk, *The Body Keeps the Score: Brain, Mind, and Body in the Healing of Trauma* (New York: Viking Penguin, 2014).
7. Daniel J. Siegel, *The Developing Mind: Toward a Neurobiology of Interpersonal Experience* (New York: Guilford Press, 1999), 13–14.
8. See Stanley H. Teitelbaum, *Illusion and Disillusionment: Core Issues in Psychotherapy* (Northvale, NJ: Jason Aronson, Inc., 1999).
9. See Van der Kolk, *Body Keeps the Score*, Part Five.
10. See Siegel, *Developing Mind.*
11. Gottman and Silver, *Seven Principles*, 2.
12. Ibid., 27–33.
13. Wendy Ulrich, *Weakness Is Not Sin: The Liberating Distinction That Awakens Our Strengths* (Salt Lake City: Deseret Book, 2009), 75–93.

Chapter 5: Gaining Compassion for the Past

1. Wikipedia, https://en.wikipedia.org/wiki/Pando_(tree).
2. See Daniel J. Siegel and Mary Hartzell, *Parenting from the Inside Out: How a Deeper Self-Understanding Can Help You Raise Children Who Thrive* (New York: Tarcher/Penguin, 2003), 122–153.
3. "I'll Go Where You Want Me to Go," *Hymns* (Salt Lake City: The Church of Jesus Christ of Latter-day Saints, 1985), no. 270.

Chapter 6: Choosing Trust for the Future

1. Bible Dictionary, "Fear," 672.
2. Anonymous, personal communication.
3. Anonymous, personal communication.
4. James A. Coan, Hillary S. Schaefer, and Richard J. Davidson, "Lending a Hand: Social Regulation of the Neural Response to Threat," *Psychological Science* 17, no. 12 (2006): 1032–39.

5. Mario Mikulincer and Phillip R. Shaver, "Boosting Attachment Security to Promote Mental Health, Prosocial Values, and Inter-Group Tolerance," *Psychological Inquiry* 18, no. 3 (2007): 143.

6. Ibid.

7. See M.P. Duke, A. Lazarus, and R. Fivush, "Knowledge of family history as a clinically useful index of psychological well-being and prognosis: A brief report," *Psychotherapy Theory, Research, Practice, Training* (2008), 45, 268–72.

8. Mikulincer and Shaver, "Boosting Attachment Security," 142.

9. Ibid., 152.

10. Ibid.

11. Marily Oppezzo and Daniel L. Schwartz, "Give Your Ideas Some Legs: The Positive Effect of Walking on Creative Thinking," *Journal of Experimental Psychology: Learning, Memory, and Cognition* 40, no. 4 (2014): 1142–52.

12. N. B. Lundwall, *Discourses on the Holy Ghost, also Lectures on Faith as Delivered at the School of the Prophets at Kirtland, Ohio* (Salt Lake City, UT: Bookcraft, 1959), 119.

Chapter 7: Practicing Stillness in the Present

1. Elizabeth Barrett Browning, lines from "Aurora Leigh" (1857).

2. http://emp.byui.edu/ANDERSONR/itc/Book%20of_Mormon/09_3nephi/3nephi17/3nephi17_07prayer_js.htm.

3. As elsewhere in this book, stories in this chapter are used with permission, but with names and identifying information changed unless last names are used.

4. *Teachings of the Prophet Joseph Smith*, selected and arranged by Joseph Fielding Smith (Salt Lake City: Deseret Book, 1976), 151.

Chapter 8: Obtaining Deliverance from Evil

1. Vincent J. Felitti et al., "Relationship of Childhood Abuse and Household Dysfunction to Many of the Leading Causes of Death in Adults: The Adverse Childhood Experiences (ACE) Study," *American Journal of Preventive Medicine* 14, no. 4: 245–58; quoted in Van der Kolk, *Body Keeps the Score*, 145.

2. Reported in Van der Kolk, *Body Keeps the Score*, 148.

3. Motoko Rich, "Percentage of Poor Students in Public School Rises," *The New York Times*, 16 January 2015, http://www.nytimes.com/2015/01/17/us/school-poverty-study-southern-education-foundation.html?_r=0.

4. M. H. van Ijzendoorn, C. Schuengel, and M. Bakermans-Kranenburg, "Disorganized Attachment in Early Childhood: Meta-analysis of Precursors, Concomitants, and Sequelae," *Development and Psychopathology* 11 (2009): 225–49; referenced in Van der Kolk, *Body Keeps the Score*, 118.

5. Lane Anderson, "One City's Answer to the High Two-Year College Dropout Rate," *Deseret News*, 9 April 2015, http://www.deseretnews .com/article/865625925/Yonkers-program-keeps-kids-in-college .html?pg=1.

6. Van der Kolk, *Body Keeps the Score*, 13.

7. S. Michael Wilcox, "The Majesty of Forgiveness," Time Out for Women address, 2015.

8. http://www.imdb.com/title/tt0083987/quotes.

9. See *Weakness Is Not Sin: The Liberating Distinction That Awakens Our Strengths* (Salt Lake City: Deseret Book, 2009); see also "It Isn't a Sin to Be Weak," *Ensign*, April 2015, 30–35.

10. "Abide with Me," *Hymns*, no. 166.

11. Anonymous, personal communication.

Chapter 9: Letting God Love Us

1. Oppezzo and Schwartz, "Give Your Ideas Some Legs."

2. *Teachings of the Presidents of the Church: Joseph Smith* (Salt Lake City: The Church of Jesus Christ of Latter-day Saints, 2007), 42.

3. See Wendy Ulrich, *The Temple Experience: Passage to Healing and Holiness* (Springville, UT: Cedar Fort, 2012), chapter 5, "The Creator's Child."

4. See Ezra Taft Benson, "What I Hope You Will Teach Your Children about the Temple," *Temples of the Church of Jesus Christ of Latter-day Saints* (The Church of Jesus Christ of Latter-day Saints, 1988), 42–43.

5. Desmond Tutu, in "Desmond Tutu, Insisting We Are 'Made for Goodness,'" NPR interview by Renee Montagne, March 11, 2010, npr.org.

6. D. Todd Christofferson, "Be at Peace," *Ensign*, December 2015, 30–31.

Appendix

1. Harville Hendrix, *Getting the Love You Want: Couples Workshop Manual* (Winter Park, FL: Imago Relationships International, 1979). Adapted with permission from Imago Relationships.

INDEX

—◦◦◦✝◦◦◦—

Abba, 18

Abraham, 121–23

Abuse, 161–62, 164, 168–70

Acceptance and Renewal Stage, 31–33, 43–45, 48, 64–66, 203

Adoption, 39–40

Advocate, Jesus Christ as, 60

Agency, 66–67, 198

Ainsworth, Mary, 81

Airplane landing, 135–36

Anxiety, 115–16, 129

Anxious attachment, 83–85, 115–16

Apostles, 153–55

Aspen grove, 98

Assumptions, faulty, 5–9, 13–17

Atonement, 75, 161

Attachment: theory of, 80–82; to God, 97; poverty's effect on, 163

Attachment style(s): questionnaire determining, 76–80; secure, 82–83; anxious, 83–85; avoidant, 85–87; traumatic, 87–88; and possibility of change, 88–90, 102–3; impact of, on view of future, 115–20

Avoidant attachment, 85–87

Blessings, temptation and, 185

Book of Mormon, lost manuscript pages of, 37–38

Bowlby, John, 80–81

Bread, 139–40

Browning, Elizabeth Barrett, 141–42

Butterfly pin, lost, ix–x

Chair, empty, 200–201

Change, 60, 88–90, 92–93, 102–3, 107–8

Child abuse, 162, 164, 168–70

Children: parents' influence on, 74–75, 76, 90–91, 100–102, 117–19, 207–10; attachment and, 80–89; expectations learned as, 100–102; protecting, 130

Children of Israel, 60–62

Christofferson, D. Todd, 201–2

Church, 194–95

"Come unto me," 54–58

Committed relationships: stages of, 25–26, 187; Honeymoon Stage, 26–28, 33, 35–36, 58–59, 203; Power Struggle Stage, 28–30, 36–38, 49, 59–62, 203; Withdrawal Stage, 30–31, 39–43, 62–64, 203; Acceptance and Renewal

Stage, 31–33, 43–45, 48, 64–66, 203; understanding, 33–34; Precommitment Stage, 52–53, 204; learning skills of emotional intimacy in, 128. *See also* Marriage
Compassion, 96, 108–11, 183–84, 185
Contempt, 95–96
Conversations, 195
Cornbread, 144–45
Covenant relationship, 15, 34
Creation, 197
Creative process, 66–67, 194
Criticism, 95–96

Debtors, forgiving, 167–70
Defensiveness, 95–96
Disobedience, 122
Doubts, 39–43, 45

Earned secure attachment, 90, 102
Eating, 192–94
Edits, lost, 109–11
Emotions, prior experiences and, 105–6
Empty chair, 200–201
Esau, 60–61
Evil: deliverance from, 159–61; effects of, 161–63; and kingdom of God, 163–67; forgiveness and deliverance from, 167–75; outside versus inside, 179; and preparing against temptation, 180–82; and controlling thoughts, 182–83; compassion as antidote to, 183–84
Expectations, 100–102

Faith, trials of, 39–43, 45
Family history, 126–27
Father, God as, 19–21
Faulty assumptions, 5–9, 13–17
Fear: of intimacy, 4; prior experiences and, 105–6; of future, 113–15, 187; of social dangers, 116–17
Feelings, prior experiences and, 105–6
File, lost, 109–11

Forgiveness, 115, 167–75, 188, 191
Future: fear of, 113–15, 187; impact of past on view of, 115–20

Gandhi, 172
Gethsemane, 18–19
God: relationship with, x–xi, 15–16, 22–24, 205–10; hard feelings against, 5; perception of, 8–9, 71, 74–75, 94–95, 118–20, 137–38, 211; getting closer to, 9–13, 94; love of, 16, 53–54, 74–76, 186–91, 204–5; receiving, 17–18; as Father, 19–21; Honeymoon Stage with, 35–36, 203; Power Struggle Stage with, 36–38, 203; Withdrawal Stage with, 39–43, 203; Acceptance and Renewal Stage with, 43–45, 203; Lehi, Laman, Lemuel, and Nephi's relationships with, 48–52; Precommitment Stage with, 52–53, 204; trust in, 53, 105, 123–38; voice of, 59–60; changing, 60; wrestling with, 61–62; working with, 66–67, 194; expectations and relationship with, 76–80, 100–102; secure attachment and relationship with, 83; anxious attachment and relationship with, 84–85; avoidant attachment and relationship with, 86–87; traumatic attachment and relationship with, 88; growing up in, 90–93, 99; toxic relationship patterns and, 95–96; attaching to, 97; perspective of, 104, 211; submission to, 113–15, 166–67; kingdom of, 114–15, 163–67; help from, 122–23; rethinking image of, 123–24; gathering, to us daily, 140–41; remembering, 141–42; sitting with, 151–53, 201–2; keeping, at distance, 186–88; desires closeness, 188–89; walking with, 192; eating with, 192–94; playing

with, 194; going to church with, 194–95; in our conversations, 195; praying with, 195–96; becoming like, 196–99; role of, in Godhead, 197

Godhead, 196–98

Grandma Mattie, 134–35

Gratitude, 144–47

Group affiliations, 127

Grudges, 173–75, 191

Hard feelings, 5

Harris, Martin, 37

Health, 162

Help, from God, 122–23

Holiness, 184–85

Holy Ghost: following, 39–40; writing down experiences with, 58; keeping presence of, 141, 190–91; role of, in Godhead, 198–99. *See also* Revelation

Holy strengths, 179

Honeymoon Stage, 26–28, 33, 35–36, 58–59, 203

Hosea, 23–24

Humility, 93–94, 96, 180–81

Intimacy: fear of, 4; and changing faulty assumptions, 5–6; controlling, with God, 14; and Withdrawal Stage, 41; tolerating, 63; learning skills of emotional, 128

Israel: as bride of Christ, 47; children of, 60–62

Israelson, Brent, 146

Israelson, Dana, 145–47

"It Is Well with My Soul," 136–37

Jacob, 60–62

Jesus Christ: prayers of, 18–19, 56–57, 161, 189; relationship with, 22–23; Israel as bride of, 47; calls people unto Him, 54–58; sacred suppers

with, 58–59; as Advocate, 60; becoming rooted in, 92–93; as Root, 98–99; and practicing attachment security, 126; recognizing, 153–55; trust in, 155, 192; remembering, 156–58, 193; joins in state of mortal weakness, 178; role of, in Godhead, 197–98

Johnny cake, 144–45

Justice, 167–70

Kingdom of God, 114–15, 163–67

Kirtland Temple, 91

Laman, 49, 50

Last Supper, 58

Lehi, 48

Lemuel, 49, 50

Liberty Jail, 41

Lord's Prayer, 71–72, 73, 100, 113, 139–40, 159

Loss, 109–11

Love: of God, 16, 53–54, 74–76, 204–5; receiving, 186–91; relearning meaning of, 189–90

Manna, 139–40, 149

Marriage: unity and connection in, 24–25; toxic relationship patterns in, 95–96. *See also* Committed relationships

Mattie, Grandma, 134–35

Maturity, spiritual, 7–8

McConkie, Bruce R., 20

Memories, and practicing attachment security, 127

Mercy, 167–70

Mindfulness, 193

Mortality: separation in, 57; weakness in, 175–79; difficulties of, 199–200

Nebraska, 40–41, 63–64

Nephi, 48–52

Obedience, 39–40
Options, searching for new, 130–32

Packer, Boyd K., 20, 26–27, 32
Pain: and spiritual maturity, 7–8;
    protecting children from, 130
Pando, 98
Parable of the sower, 92
Parents: influence of, on relationship
    with God, 74–75, 76, 100–102,
    117–19, 207–10; attachment and,
    81–89; learning from, 90–91
Past, 102–4, 115–20, 187
Perfection, 74, 75, 76
Personal revelation, 39–40, 147–50
Perspective, 103, 104, 211
Physical closeness, 126
Plane landing, 135–36
Play, 194
Poverty, 162–63
Power Struggle Stage, 28–30, 36–38,
    49, 59–62, 203
Prayer(s): purpose of, x; of author,
    9–13, 63, 109–11; kinds of, 14;
    practicing, 15; of Jesus Christ,
    18–19, 56–57, 161, 189; following
    answers to, 39–40; developing
    relationship with God through,
    72; and rethinking image of God,
    123–24; for safe plane landing,
    135–36; for something better,
    144–45; temptation and, 180;
    with God, 195–96; writing, 205;
    suggestions for, 211
Precommitment Stage, 52–53, 204
Present, living in, 140–41, 142–44,
    146–47, 150–51, 156
Promised Land, 48, 51, 52

Rachel, 138
Receiving, 17–18
Redemption, 99–100, 200
Regrafting, 93–94

Relationships: with God, x–xi, 15–16,
    22–24; influence of, 3–4; spiritual
    maturity in, 7–8; building, 15–16;
    tolerating vulnerability and intimacy
    in, 63; impact of early, 72–76;
    understanding predispositions in,
    76–80; humility in, 93–94; toxic,
    95–96; evil's impact on, 164–66;
    patterns in, 207–10. See also
    Attachment style(s); Committed
    relationships
Remembering, 18–19
Repentance, 176, 191
Resilience, 126–27, 132–33, 190, 200,
    211
Resourcefulness, 126–27
Restitution, 172
Revelation, 39–40, 147–50
Root, Jesus Christ as, 98–99

Sacrament, 58, 156–58, 193, 195, 211
Satan: voice of, 59–60; and avoiding
    trials, 120, 122; tactics of, 164, 198;
    overcoming, 166
Secure attachment, 82–83, 116–17,
    124–29; earned, 90, 102
Self-compassion, 90, 96
Self-recrimination, 173–75, 191
Shame, 180, 183
Sin, 164–65, 175–77, 191. See also
    Forgiveness
Skarda, Carrie, 193
Skills, developing, 127
Smith, John Lyman, 144–45
Smith, Joseph: and lost Book of
    Mormon manuscript pages, 37–38;
    in Liberty Jail, 41; trusting in, 44;
    and Kirtland Temple dedication, 91;
    prays for something better, 144–45;
    on revelation, 148; on Godhead, 196
Social dangers, fear of, 116–17
Souvenirs, and practicing attachment
    security, 127
Sower, parable of, 92

Spiritual experiences: recording, 58; and avoiding trials, 120–22

Spiritual maturity, 7–8

Spiritual progress, 66–67

Spirit world, 112

Stokes, James G., 16

Stonewalling, 95–96

Story, versus history, 102–4

Strengths, holy, 179

Suffering, 8, 55, 79, 121–22, 169, 198, 199–200. *See also* Trials

Support, asking for, 131–32

Talents, developing, 127

Temple work, 91

Temptation, 180–83, 185, 211

Thoughts, controlling, 182–83

Threats, social, 116–17

Toxic relationships, 95–96

Trauma, 164–65

Traumatic attachment, 87–88, 115–16

Tree of life vision, 49–50

Trials: learning from, 108, 133–38; avoiding, 120–23; dealing with, 142–44. *See also* Suffering

Trials of faith, 39–43, 45

Trust: in Joseph Smith, 44; in God, 53, 105, 190; in redemption, 99–100; in your own resilience, 132–33, 190; in Jesus Christ, 155, 192

Tutu, Bishop Desmond, 201

Veil, seeing beyond, 112

Vietnam vet, 164–65, 171

Visiting teaching, 147, 148

Vulnerability, 4, 8, 63, 181

Walking, 131, 192

Weakness, 175–79, 191

Wickedness, 122

Wilcox, S. Michael, 170

Will of God, accepting, 113–15

Withdrawal Stage, 30–31, 39–43, 62–64, 203

Work, 153–55, 194

ABOUT THE AUTHOR

WENDY ULRICH, PhD, MBA, has been a psychologist in private practice, president of the Association of Mormon Counselors and Psychotherapists, and a visiting professor at Brigham Young University–Provo. She founded Sixteen Stones Center for Growth, which offers seminar-retreats for Latter-day Saint women and their loved ones (see sixteenstones.net). Her books include *Weakness Is Not Sin*; *Habits of Happiness*; *The Temple Experience*; *Forgiving Ourselves*; and national best-seller *The Why of Work*, co-authored with her husband, Dave Ulrich.